VEGETARIAN NOSH FOR STUDENTS

by Joy May and the family team

THE NOSH SERIES OF COOKBOOKS BY JOY MAY

NOSH FOR STUDENTS — 5TH EDITION — A FUN STUDENT COOKBOOK — JOY MAY

ISBN: 9780993260933

NOSH FOR STUDENTS — VOL.2 — JOY MAY

ISBN: 9780956746467

VEGETARIAN NOSH FOR STUDENTS — A FUN STUDENT COOKBOOK — JOY MAY

ISBN: 9780993260940

NOSH QUICK & EASY — JOY MAY

ISBN: 9780956746481

NOSH FOR BUSY MUMS & DADS — JOY MAY

ISBN: 9780956746443

NOSH GLUTEN-FREE — JOY MAY

ISBN: 9780956746450

NOSH GLUTEN-FREE BAKING — JOY MAY

ISBN: 9780956746498

NOSH SUGAR-FREE GLUTEN-FREE — JOY MAY

ISBN: 9780993260919

@NOSHBOOKS

WE WOULD LOVE TO HEAR FROM YOU. USE #NOSHBOOKS

contents

the basics   4

fast food   38

broke but hungry   54

one-pot dishes   68

something mum might cook   88

something for the weekend   106

friends around   126

comfort food   154

date night   162

cakes and cookies   172

desserts   190

weekly food planners   200

index   204

Introduction

I am excited about getting young people to cook good, healthy meals from non-processed food sources. This edition of Vegetarian Nosh for Students is packed with yummy recipes and ideas for vegetarian students.

Having had two sons go through Uni, I know the restrictions and hazards of student kitchens. With this in mind, I have made the book as straightforward as possible. At the same time, I have introduced a good variety of ingredients to give vegetarians a healthy, balanced diet and, possibly, to introduce them to some new foodstuffs.

Cooking vegetarian food requires a little more thinking 'out of the box', or you will end up eating the same cheese on toast or stir-fry all the time. This book aims to inspire to greater heights.

The layout makes cooking easy and inspiring: there is a photo of each recipe that should help. There are also some weekly menu and shopping plans.

The recipes are planned so that you need to use the minimum of pans, dishes and utensils. You need use no weighing scales. There is also a list of stuff you need to take to uni to help you cook.

Simple Key

How much it will cost per person.

How easy it is to make. 1 star being super-easy and 5 stars more adventurous.

How many people the recipe will feed.

How long it will take to prepare the meal.

How long it takes to cook the food (oven or hob).

How long you might have to leave the food to cool in the fridge or freezer.

£0.80 /PERSON

3

2

PREP 15 MINS

COOK 20 MINS

COOL 2 HRS

Recipe costs

The recipe costs in this book are an average between Tesco and Sainsbury's and are the prices at the time of writing. To keep the pricing very relevant, we will update each new print run. Last update **Feb 2017**.

One of the key features of this book is that you do not need weighing scales and special measuring equipment. These things are not usually found in student accommodation.

Throughout the book I have used a mug to measure ingredients. This mug holds 1/2 a pint of liquid and is the size of the mug pictured opposite.

a mug =

ACTUAL SIZE

The following is all you will need to be able to cook every recipe in this book:

- ☑ mug (approx. ½ pint)
- ☑ tablespoon, one mum serves with
- ☑ dessertspoon, one you eat cereal with
- ☑ teaspoon, one you stir tea with
- ☑ wooden spoon
- ☑ chopping board
- ☑ sharp knife
- ☑ small pan with lid
- ☑ medium-sized pan, with lid
- ☑ slotted turner (fish slice)
- ☑ frying pan
- ☑ wok is useful, but not essential
- ☑ casserole dish, with lid
- ☑ colander
- ☑ flat roasting dish, or metal non-stick cooking tray
- ☑ cheese grater
- ☑ hand-held blender
- ☑ sieve
- ☑ loaf tin
- ☑ mixing bowl

Good buying ideas

It is good to **plan a menu for the week.** This makes cooking much easier, since you will not be dashing to the shops the whole time for little things. It also means you will not waste food, as you will just buy what you need for the week. Try the planner on the opposite page.

Look at page 12. **Make sure that you are getting a balanced diet.** Decide before you go to the shops what kind of vegetables and fruits you need to buy. Fruit and veg are best eaten when fresh, because the minerals and vitamins deteriorate after 2–3 days.

Always make sure that, when you have visited home, you return to uni having **creamed off any 'excess'** from mum's cupboards.

You will need to **build up a stock of herbs and spices** in order to keep your food tasty and varied. Buy in bulk from Asian supermarkets: they cost a fraction of the price. Keep them in sealed packets, or jars, and they will maintain their flavour for a long time.

Nuts and dried fruits are sometimes cheaper in places like **Holland and Barrett and Julian Graves.**

If you are sharing accommodation with other vegetarians, **share the cooking with them**. You cook one day and they the next. This will not only save you time and hassle, but cooking in larger quantities will save you money in the long run.

weekly Food planner

This plan assumes that you will eat sandwiches and fruit for lunch each day and cereal or toast for breakfast.

This menu should cost about **£16 for the week.**

Menu

Monday Spag Bol p108

Tuesday Rest of Spag Bol

Wednesday Baked Potato and Cheese p24

Thursday Sweet Potato Patties p93

Friday Rest of Sweet Potato

Saturday 1/2 quantity of French Onion Soup p55

Sunday Classic Nut Roast - share with a friend p156

Shopping List
- cereal for breakfast
- milk
- bread for sandwiches
- sandwich fillings
- 2 medium sweet potatoes
- 1 large potato
- 3 onions
- 2 mushrooms
- 1 carrot
- 1 head of celery
- 1 red pepper
- 1 small lettuce
- 1 tomato
- 1 tin tomatoes
- 1 small tin sweetcorn
- 1 packet spaghetti
- Parmesan-style cheese
- 250g Cheddar cheese
- 1 small carton fromage frais
- 1 small carton natural yogurt
- 200g pack cashew nuts
- 1 leek
- fresh ginger
- 1 lemon
- 2 spring onions
- 1 small cucumber

check cupboards for:
- oil
- stock cubes
- oregano
- Marmite
- sugar
- red lentils
- garlic
- honey
- mixed herbs

For more weekly food plans see pages 200-203

Storecupboard and Fridge

Here are some basics to keep in your storecupboard and fridge. Usually in student halls, or shared houses, you will have a shelf in the fridge, one drawer in the freezer and a cupboard to yourself.

FRIDGE/FREEZER

spare loaf of bread in freezer
spare pint of milk in freezer
(plastic not glass bottles)
butter/spread
milk
eggs
cheese
mayo
curry paste
Quorn

STORECUPBOARD

rice
pasta
cereal
tin of chopped tomatoes
tin of baked beans
tins of beans and pulses
dried lentils and pulses
tofu
pilau rice seasoning (livens up rice)
soy sauce
curry paste (put in fridge once open)
oil to cook with
salt and pepper
vegetable stock cubes
cornflour
tomato purée
Marmite
sugar
flour
cornflour
useful herbs and spices
mixed dried herbs
dried basil
chilli flakes
paprika

Good things to eat

You will know, as a vegetarian, that it is important for you to think carefully about the food you eat. Eating loads of pasta, cheese and vegetables is not really sufficient. There are many good sources of proteins, vitamins and minerals to be found. Below are some general guidelines to eating healthily as a vegetarian.

RECOMMENDED DAILY INTAKE:
(NOTE, ONE PORTION = ONE SERVING OR 1 PIECE FRUIT)

3–4	portions of cereals, grains, or potatoes
4–5	portions of fruit, or vegetables (1 glass of real fruit juice counts as 1 portion)
2–3	portions of pulses, nuts, or seeds
2	portions of milk, cheese, eggs, or soya
A small quantity	vegetable oil, butter, or margarine

Carbohydrates. These are our main energy source. However, too much carbohydrate is not good for you. Sources include bread, white rice, potatoes and other root vegetables, pasta, flour, cereal, sweets and chocolate.

Proteins. These are 'body builders', not just to develop muscle, but to keep our cartilage, hair, skin and blood in good shape. Sources include dairy products, grains, cereals, pulses, seeds, nuts, Quorn, tofu and eggs.

Fats. We do need some fat in our diet, but it is essential not to overdo it. Eat fats which are high in monounsaturated and polyunsaturated fats.

Vitamins and Minerals. If you eat a balanced diet, you will get the vitamins and minerals you need. Milk is an excellent balanced food. Milk is rich in minerals, vitamins and calcium and is also high in protein, carbohydrate and fat. Skimmed or semi-skimmed is the best. You need to make sure you get enough iron, in order to keep your blood count healthy. Iron is found in some unrefined cereals, pulses, beans and lentils. Fruit, vegetables and nuts provide a wide range of vitamins and minerals.

Soya and microproteins. Soya is a vegetable protein and contains amino acids (good for you). Soya beans are low in cholesterol and unsaturated fats and high in calcium. Sources: soya milk, soya sauce, textured vegetable protein (TVP) and tofu. Tofu contains calcium, iron and vitamins B1, B2 and B3.

Fruit and Vegetables. Provide fibre, essential in our diet, together with vitamins and minerals. Root vegetables, potatoes, carrots, swedes, etc. are not good in excess, as they are high in carbohydrates. Fresh and dried fruit and fruit smoothies make excellent, high nutrition, snacks.

Spirulina is known as a modern 'superfood'. It is known to significantly increase energy and stamina levels, as well as boost the immune system. It is an excellent food supplement for vegetarians. Buy on-line, or Holland and Barrett.

If, on any one day, you choose to make a dish that has only vegetables, make sure that you eat some soya, nuts and/or cheese. Have fresh and dried fruit and nuts to hand and get into the habit of eating them. If, by the end of the week, you have fruit that needs eating, make a smoothie!

Things to look out for

If you are new to being vegetarian, it is easy to accidentally eat things that contain traces of meat product. Listed opposite are some potential pitfalls relevant to the recipes in this book.

See www.vegsoc.org for an extended list.

Health food shops are good places to source vegetarian foods. The staff know what they are talking about. Nuts and dried fruits are usually much cheaper there than in the supermarkets.

When shopping, read the labels carefully. You will soon find good sources of vegetarian foods. Look for Vegetarian Society approved products.

POTENTIAL PITFALLS

Additives/ E numbers	certain additives in foods may not be vegetarian, for example, cochineal is sometimes present in glacé cherries. Buy cochineal-free cherries.
Bread	some bakers may grease the tins with animal fat, check your local baker.
Butter	make sure you buy pure butter.
Cheese	may have been produced using animal rennet. Look for vegetarian alternatives.
Chocolate	can contain whey and emulsifiers, check the labels.
Crisps	the flavourings may contain whey. Some crisps may be made with yeast extract.
Curry paste	Thai curry paste may contain fish or fish sauce. Indian curry pastes are usually OK.
Egg noodles	make sure they are made from free-range eggs, or look for eggless noodles, e.g. rice noodles.
Eggs	we recommend that you only use free-range eggs.
Gelatine	made from animal source, sometimes in sweets and desserts.
GM foods	are to be avoided.
Margarines	may contain animal fats or fish oils. Buy olive oil spreads.
Mayonnaise	may contain eggs which are not free-range. Check labels or look for vegetarian variety.
Parmesan cheese	is usually not vegetarian. Look for a Parmesan-style vegetarian cheese.
Pasta	may not be made with free-range eggs. Check the label.
Stock	buy vegetarian and make sure does not contain animal fats.
Tofu	can sometimes be GM.
Wine vinegars, alcohol & juices	may be refined with a non-vegetarian source. Read labels carefully.
Yogurts, cream & crème fraîche	some of these may contain gelatine.
Flour	may contain 'flour improvers', that could come from animal sources.

How long can I keep this before it kills me?

HOW LONG CAN I KEEP THINGS?

Eggs	1 month from lay date (usually the use-by date on the egg).
Milk	2–3 days once opened. If unopened see 'best-before' date.
Butter and margarine	6 weeks
Cheese	1 week once opened, 2 weeks unopened. Keep cheese wrapped.
Onions and potatoes	1 week, best out of the fridge and in a dark place.
Green vegetables	1 week in fridge.
Carrots, parsnips, etc.	1 week in fridge.
Salad, lettuce, cucumber, tomatoes, peppers, etc.	1 week in fridge.
Leftovers	ONLY the day after the food has been cooked. All kinds of 'nasties' can begin to lurk there.

Sell-by dates are dates by which the store needs to sell things. **Use-by dates** are indications that you should not be eating them after said date.

Here are some basic guidelines that should help you avoid making yourself ill:

HOW DO I KNOW IF SOMETHING IS PAST IT?

Cheese	Green mould on the surface.
Potatoes	Skin is turning green and excessive 'ears'.
Yogurts	Lid 'puffing up'. If opened, the smell changes and it tastes 'sharp'.
Bread	Mould around the crust.
Vegetables	Originally crisp vegetables, now soft and soggy, e.g. 'bendy' carrots.

Reheating food

Take care when reheating food, that you **heat it thoroughly.** It should be 'piping hot'. This means all the food should be steaming and the plate needs a cloth to get it out of the microwave.

To reheat a plate of food in the microwave, **cover it with cling film and place on a high heat** for approximately 3½ mins in a 600watt microwave. However, refer to the point above if you are unsure.

Storing stuff

A few plastic, sealable boxes and some cling film are essentials when sharing a fridge while you are in halls or house sharing. If you share with those who eat meat or keep unacceptable stuff in the fridge, keep things wrapped and your food should stay OK.

If you cook a meal one day, **eat any leftovers the next day** and not after that.

Be very careful with rice. Cool it quickly and place it in the fridge.

Don't keep opened tins in the fridge; a chemical reaction occurs affecting the food once the tin is open to the air. Transfer any excess to a bowl and cover with cling film.

Keep potatoes out of the fridge in a cool, dark place. This can be inside a cupboard and stops them going green so quickly.

Nuts and dried fruits—invest in a packet of clothes-pegs and seal any opened packets with them. If you have the room, keep them all in a large, plastic box.

Seven steps to success

Here are some things that will help you enjoy cooking and hopefully minimise discouraging failures.

1 Plan what you will eat, and shop for the week all in one go. This saves time and money, as you will not buy stuff you don't need. At the back of the book you will find sample menus for a week. Once you are used to using these, you can make your own menus and shopping lists.

2 Try to keep things varied, e.g. don't cook the same stir-fry over and over again. Try new recipes and gradually stock up on the more unusual ingredients.

3 When frying vegetables, especially onions, make sure you take the time to allow them to brown. This caramelises the starches and sugars in the food, and gives them a much better taste.

4 Try to keep things clean in the kitchen, e.g. chopping boards, dish cloths and tea towels. Even though you are not dealing with meat yourself, if others in the kitchen are, then you need to take extra care.

5 Prepare all the ingredients before you begin to cook. For example, don't try to chop vegetables whilst you are frying other things.

6 Read the recipe all the way through, before you begin, in order to get a clear idea of what you are doing.

7 Start by cooking the easy things you know and like, if you are not a confident cook.

What do I do if...

...everything I cook in the oven is burnt or undercooked?

It could be that, if you have an older oven, the thermostat is not working quite as well as it should. Don't give up, just adjust by raising or lowering the temperature you set it to. Also, the temperatures in some ovens can vary a great deal, depending on which shelf you put your food on. Where possible, use middle shelves. Check what kind of oven you have: Centigrade, Centigrade fan oven or Fahrenheit oven. Then check the temperature on the recipe.

...I don't have a microwave to defrost food?

Keep the food in the freezer bag and place in cold water, don't use boiling water. The best thing is to plan ahead, take food out of the freezer and leave in the fridge overnight to defrost.

...I don't have a lid for my casserole dish?

Cover it with foil and scrunch the edges to seal to the dish.

...sauces go lumpy?

Put them in a jug or bowl and whizz them with a hand-held blender.

...everything I cook on top of the cooker is burnt?

Either you need to keep the heat turned down, or just keep an eye on things. You can't go off and ring your mates, whilst trying to cook.

...I have made things too spicy?

With chilli dishes, just try adding another tin of tomatoes. With a curry, peel and cut a potato into four and add to the curry, simmer for 10 minutes and remove potato.

...everything seems tasteless?

Remember to season well as you cook.

Veggies

Boiling

Generally, most vegetables need to be cooked in just enough water to cover them.

1. Bring the water to the boil.
2. Once boiling, add the vegetables and a little salt and simmer gently, with the lid on the pan. If you keep the source of the heat low, you will preserve a little more of the nutrition in the vegetables.

BOILING TIMES

Swedes and turnips	2–3cm chunks	20–25 mins
Potatoes	2–3cm chunks	10–15 mins
Parsnips, carrots	cut into 2cm rings	10–15 mins
Cauliflower	broken into little trees	10 mins
Broccoli	broken into little trees	5 mins
Green beans	cut off the stalk and tail	5 mins
Spinach	take off any thick stalks	30 secs–1 min
Leeks	cut into 2cm rings	5 mins
Cabbage	cut into long thin strips	5 mins
Sugar snaps	leave as they are	2 mins
Mangetout	leave as they are	1 min

Note

For **spinach**, cook just enough to make the leaves wilt. You will only need a quarter of a mug of water in the bottom of the pan.

For **cabbage**, use half a mug of water in the pan, drain after cooking and add some butter and black pepper. Return to the pan and cook for another 2 minutes to dry the cabbage a little.

Roasting

1. Preheat the oven to 180°C fan oven/200°C/Gas 6.

2. Put the vegetables on a flat roasting/baking tray and sprinkle them with salt and olive oil. Turn them over with your hands, to make sure that the oil is covering all the pieces. Set them on the tray with flat sides up. If the flat sides are on the tray itself, they will tend to stick. Sprinkle with rosemary if you wish.

3. Put in the middle of the oven for 30 minutes. Check to see if any are getting too brown, maybe the ones around the edge. Move, or turn over as necessary. Put back in the oven for another 20 minutes. You can put a mix of veg in (see photo below). If you are roasting individual veg, see timings below:

ROASTING TIMES

Potatoes	cut into 5–6cm chunks	40–50 mins
Butternut squash	peel, cut into 5–6cm chunks	30–40 mins
Parsnips	cut into 4, lengthways	40–45 mins
Sweet potatoes	peel, cut into 5–6cm chunks	40–50 mins
Onions	cut into 6 wedges	40–50 mins
Fennel	cut into 4 wedges	30–40 mins
Tomatoes	cut the skin	20–25 mins
Peppers	remove seeds and stalk, cut into large pieces	25 mins

Perfect rice every time

There are many different types of rice to buy. I would recommend that you use basmati. It is slightly more expensive than long grain or quick-cook rice, but has a much better flavour and texture than the cheaper varieties.

rice for 1 person = ½ mug rice + 1 mug water

(+ 1 teaspoon of pilau rice seasoning, optional, but gives a yummy flavour.)

1. Using a pan with a lid, bring the water to the boil, add the seasoning and stir until it has dissolved.

2. Add the rice and stir once, bring back to the boil. Once boiling, turn down the heat to very low, so that the rice simmers gently. Put the lid on the pan and cook for approximately 15 minutes. Do not stir whilst the rice is cooking, or you will make it sticky. The rice should be cooked once the water has disappeared. Check occasionally to see if the water has boiled away.

3. Test the rice once the water has boiled away. If the rice is still too crunchy and the water has all gone, then you have boiled it too quickly. Add a little more water, replace the lid and cook for another 5 minutes.

Joy did a video of this, check it out at noshbooks.com/rice

How to cook pasta

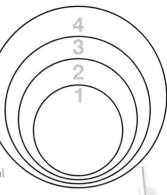

4
3
2
1

There are innumerable kinds of pasta to choose from in the shops, made from different ingredients. Most will have instructions on the packets as to how to cook them. Just in case you have lost the packet, here are some general guidelines:

Spaghetti

1. Use the guide above to measure the quantities required for 1–4 people. Boil sufficient water in a pan to cover the spaghetti whilst cooking.

2. Once the water is boiling, lower the spaghetti sticks into the water. Once the half that is in the water has softened slightly, push the other half in. Simmer for 6–8 minutes.

3. Test one piece to see if it is cooked. Drain the water off and add one teaspoon of butter or olive oil. Mix around and this will stop the spaghetti sticking together.

Most other pastas

Again, boil enough water to cover the pasta. Once the water is boiling, add the pasta. **One mug of dried pasta is plenty for one person with a very healthy appetite.** Simmer for the appropriate time, drain and add butter or olive oil to prevent the pasta sticking together.

Here is a guide, but it still depends on the thickness of the pasta:
Tagliatelle - the stuff that comes in little nests. 4–5 minutes.
Spaghetti - 6 minutes, depending how thick the spaghetti is.
Radiatore - looks like little radiators. 10 minutes.
Fusilli - little twists. 6–8 minutes.
Penne - little tubes, vary in size. 10–12 minutes.
Conchiglie - little shells. 6–8 minutes.
Macaroni - 12–15 minutes.
Farfalle - looks like little bows. 6–8 minutes.

Jacket Potatoes

Use medium or large potatoes. Always make a cut in the skin with a knife before baking, or it may explode in the oven or the microwave. You will only get the crisp jackets if you cook potatoes in the oven. Timing depends on the size of the potato.

Oven baked — Preheat the oven to 200°C fan oven/220°C/Gas 7, bake for 50–60 minutes.
Microwave and oven — Preheat the oven to 200°C fan oven/220°C/Gas 7. Cook in the microwave on full power for 5 minutes and then in the oven for 30 minutes.
Microwave — 7–10 minutes on full power.

Fillings

When the potato is cooked, cut it open and add a little butter to moisten, then add any of the following suggestions:

1 **The Simplest**—Baked beans and/or grated cheese.

2 **Cheesy Chives**—Mix together ½ x 125g packet of soft cream cheese, 2 dessertspoons fromage frais, 2 x 2cm cubes of blue cheese, crumbled, 1 stick of finely chopped celery, 1 teaspoon chives and 2 chopped spring onions. Season with salt and pepper. (You can vary this recipe using different kinds of cheese, strong ones are best.)

3 **Twice Baked Potato, with Pesto**—Cut the baked potato in half, lengthways. Scoop out the soft potato with a spoon, being careful not to break the skin. Place in a dish and mash with a fork. Mix in 1 tablespoon of thick double cream, 1 teaspoon of vegetarian green pesto sauce, a squeeze of lemon juice and one teaspoon of pine nuts. Season with salt and pepper. Put the potato mixture back into the skin and grate some Parmesan-style cheese over the top. Return to the oven for 20 minutes until the cheese has browned.

4 **Egg and Mayo and Sweetcorn**—Hard boil 2 eggs (see page 30). Peel off the shell and roughly chop. Add 1 tablespoon of mayonnaise, half a small tin of sweetcorn and season well with salt and pepper.

5 **Cheese and Mushroom**—Finely chop a small garlic clove and fry in a little butter for 30 seconds. Add 3 sliced mushrooms and ½ teaspoon of dried mixed herbs. Cook for 1 minute. Take off the heat and add a good tablespoon of cream cheese. Season well.

6 **Roasted Veg**—Peel a sweet potato, cut into 2 cm chunks, ½ red pepper, cut into 8 pieces, 1 finely chopped garlic glove, ½ an onion, chopped, 1 tomato, cut into 4, and 3–4 black olives. Place on a baking tray and drizzle over with oil. Season well, mix together and place in the oven 30 minutes before the potato is cooked.

sandwiches interesting sandwiches
sandwiches interesting sandwiches
sandwiches interesting sandwiches
sandwiches interesting sandwiches
sandwiches interesting sandwiches
sandwiches interesting sandwiches
sandwiches interesting sandwiches
sandwiches interesting sandwiches
sandwiches interesting sandwiches
sandwiches interesting sandwiches
sandwiches interesting sandwiches

It is important to eat good bread, so look out for granary and wholemeal. Try not to eat white bread all the time. Pitta bread will hold a bit more filling; iceberg lettuce works well as a filling, because it gives a crispy contrast to the pitta.

Poached egg and wilted spinach

Heat a small amount of oil in a frying pan, add a large handfull of spinach and cook for 30 seconds. The spinach will wilt. Set to one side while you poach an egg (see page 30). Put together in the sandwich and season well.

Scrambled eggs and cheese and tomato

Grate 1/2 mug cheese. Chop a tomato quite finely. Heat a little butter in a small non-stick saucepan, add the tomatoes and fry for 1 minute. Add 2 eggs and cook until they begin to set. Add the cheese and cook for 30 seconds. Season well and make the sandwich while the eggs are still hot.

Egg mayo

Hard boil 2 eggs (see page 30). Rinse them under cold water, take off the shells and chop them up with a knife. Mix them together with 1 tablespoon mayo and season with salt and pepper.

Cream cheese and banana

Spread one slice of the bread with a good helping of cream cheese. Slice a banana and place on top. Spread the other slice of bread with honey or jam and press together lightly.

Feta cheese

Crumble the cheese and add iceberg lettuce, sliced tomatoes, some chopped-up spring onions and a dessertspoon of mayo.

Pistachio hummus

See page 141 for hummus recipe and add cucumber in chunky slices.

Stuff on toast

Cheese on toast
with a little something extra.

1. Very lightly toast the bread under a hot grill, since you will return it to the grill later to cook the cheese.

2. Butter the toast. At this stage you can add things to go under the cheese, such as pickle, Marmite, or sliced tomatoes.

3. Slice or grate the cheese and place on top. Make sure the cheese covers the edges of the toast; it will protect the corners of the bread from being burned. Place under the grill until browned.

Eggie bread

1. Break an egg into a mug and beat with a fork. Pour out onto a plate.

2. Dip one side of a thick slice of bread into the egg, quickly turn over and let the other side soak up the rest of the egg.

3. Put a 2cm cube of butter in a frying pan and heat gently until the butter starts to bubble.

4. Add the bread and cook, turning over to brown both sides.

5. Serve with beans, HP or tomato sauce. To make it into breakfast, serve with honey, or maple syrup.

Beans on toast with egg on top
Toast the bread, heat the beans, and then fry or poach the eggs (page 30). Great with HP sauce.

Welsh Rarebit
1/2 mug grated **Cheddar cheese**
2 teaspoons **flour**
1/2 mug **milk**
1/2 teaspoon **mustard**
1/2 teaspoon **HP Sauce**
1 **egg yolk**
2cm cube **butter**

1. Without the heat on, put the grated cheese and the flour in a small saucepan and mix well.

2. Add the rest of the ingredients and mix well.

3. Heat slowly until the mixture thickens and is hot. Serve on a thick slice of toast.

Garlic bread
Use a medium-sized baggette.

1. Finely chop 1 garlic clove, and mix together with 3cm cube of butter and 1 teaspoon of dried chives.

2. Make diagonal cuts in the bread stick, but not quite all the way through.

3. Push the garlic butter into the cuts in the bread.

4. Wrap the bread stick in foil and bake in the oven for 7-8 minutes (200°C fan oven/220°C/Gas 7).

Eggs

Boil

1. Fill a small pan ²/₃ full with water and bring to the boil.

2. Lower the egg into the pan on a spoon.

3. Simmer briskly for 3 minutes for a very runny egg, 5 minutes and you will still be able to dip your soldiers in the runny yolk, 12 minutes and it will be hard-boiled.

Poach

1. Using a frying pan, half fill with water and add a good pinch of salt. Bring to the boil, then turn down, until the water is only just moving.

2. Break the egg into a mug or cup, gently pour into the water. Do not stir or turn the heat up, just let it cook gently. It will take 2–4 minutes, depending on the size of the egg.

3. Once the egg has gone opaque, gently lift out with a slotted turner and let the water drain from it.

Fry

1. Heat 2 teaspoons butter in a frying pan, until the butter just bubbles.

2. Break the egg into a mug and then gently pour into the frying pan.

3. Cook on medium/low heat, until the egg is set.

4. Using a slotted turner, turn the egg over half-way through cooking if you want 'easy over' hard yolk.

Scramble

1. In a small milk pan, preferably non-stick, gently heat 2 teaspoons butter, until it bubbles.

2. Break the egg into the pan and season. Stir slowly, breaking up the egg yolk.

3. When the egg is almost set, take off the heat. The egg will continue to cook in its own heat. If you cook it too long it will become rubbery.

4. You can add grated cheese and/or chopped tomatoes half-way through the cooking.

Omelettes

Instructions for a basic omelette for 1 person

1. Put two or three eggs in a mug and beat well with a fork, add two tablespoons of water.

2. Preheat the grill to full heat.

3. Melt a dessertspoon of butter in a frying pan. Once it begins to 'bubble' pour the egg mixture into the pan.

4. As the egg begins to set on the bottom of the pan, gently move the set egg with fish slice and allow the runny egg to take its place. Do this with two or three sweeping movements, don't stir, or you will get scrambled egg.

5. While there is still runny egg on the top, take off the heat, add the filling you want, top with cheese (not essential) and place the frying pan under the hot grill. The omelette should rise. Once it is browned on the top, remove from the grill and turn out onto a plate. Serve with salad, garlic bread or baked potatoes.

Suggested fillings – tomato, mushrooms, fried onions, chopped spring onions, wilted spinach (page 20), or any combination of these ingredients.

Here are a few different sauces that you can use to enhance meals. All will keep in the fridge for a couple of days.

Sweet and Sour Sauce

2 tablespoons **tomato purée**

3 tablespoons **sugar**

2 tablespoons **white wine vinegar**

1 tablespoon **soy sauce**

2 teaspoons **cornflour**

1 mug **water**

1. Mix the cornflour and the water in a saucepan until smooth.
2. Add the rest of the ingredients and bring to the boil. The sauce should thicken.

Rich Tomato Sauce

1 tablespoon of **oil** to fry

1 **onion**, sliced

400g **tin tomatoes**

1 teaspoon **ground black pepper**

1 tablespoon **tomato purée**

1 tablespoon **white wine vinegar**

1 teaspoon **sugar**

1. Heat the oil in a saucepan, add the onions and fry until soft
2. Add the rest of the ingredients and bring to the boil. Simmer for 2–3 minutes. Season with salt and pepper.
3. Blitz with a hand-held blender if you have one, or use as it is.

1½ **red peppers**, chopped

½ **onion**, sliced

1 **clove garlic**, chopped

1 tablespoon **cream**

½ teaspoon **sugar**

½ **chilli powder**

1. Fry the peppers, onions, and garlic in a saucepan, over a medium heat, for 5–8 minutes, until they are really soft.
2. Add the chilli powder, sugar and cream, then mix.
3. Use the hand-held blender to liquidise, or leave as it is.
4. Add the cream, and season well with salt and freshly ground black pepper.

Quick Cheese Sauce

1 mug grated **cheese**
1 tablespoon **flour**
1/8 teaspoon **paprika**

2cm cube **butter**
1 mug **milk**

1. In a small saucepan, without the heat on, mix the grated cheese, flour, and paprika. Season.
2. Add the milk and butter. Put on a low heat and bring to the boil, stirring all the time. The sauce should thicken.

Tomato Sauce

1 tablespoon **oil** to fry
1 **onion**, chopped
1 clove **garlic**, finely chopped
1 tin **chopped tomatoes**
2 teaspoons **tomato purée**

1 teaspoon **sugar**
1 teaspoon **herbs**
1 **vegetable stock cube**, crumbled
1/4 mug **water**

1. Fry the onions and garlic in oil for 4-5 minutes.
2. Add the rest of the ingredients and bring to the boil. Turn down to simmer for 10 minutes.
3. Whizz with a blender, if you wish - we didn't!

Peanut Sauce

2 tablespoons crunchy **peanut butter**
1 dessertspoon **soy sauce**
6 tablespoons **coconut milk**

1 teaspoon **tomato purée**
1 teaspoon **sugar**

1. Mix everything together and you are ready to go!

Smoothies

You will need a hand-held blender and a jug to blend the fruits in. Once you have had a go at these ones, experiment with your own variations

Serves: 1–2 people

Melon, strawberries and yogurt

¼ of a **melon**
6–7 **strawberries**
1 tablespoon **yogurt**.

Cut up all the fruit and add to the yogurt and whizz in a jug.

Oranges

grated rind and flesh of an **orange**
1 **eating apple**, peeled and chopped
apple juice

Whizz together and add enough juice to make a drinking consistency.

Strawberries

a handful of **strawberries**
1 tablespoon of **strawberry yogurt**
a few drops of **vanilla extract**
a little **apple juice**, or **milk**.

Whizz together and add enough juice, or milk, to make a drinking consistency.

Banana, honey and yogurt

1 **banana**
2 tablespoons **yogurt**
1 dessertspoon **honey**
apple juice

Whizz together and add enough apple juice to bring to a drinking consistency.

Summer fruits

Keep a pack of frozen summer fruits in your freezer.

2 tablespoons **summer fruits**
1 tablespoon of **yogurt**
orange juice or **apple juice**

Whizz together and add enough juice to bring to a drinking consistency.

Salad dressings

Making your own salad dressings saves a heap of money and it is so satisfying. Store any excess in a sealed jar or bottle (or washed-out jam jar).

Coconut dressing

1 tablespoon **oil**
1/2 teaspoon **curry paste**
1/2 mug **coconut milk**
juice of 1/2 **lemon**
1 teaspoon **sugar**

1. Heat the oil in a small pan, add the curry paste and cook for 30 seconds on a low heat.
2. Take off the heat and mix together with the rest of the ingredients.

Creamy paprika dressing

1 teaspoon **sugar**
2 teaspoons **paprika**
4 tablespoons **white wine vinegar**
1 **egg**
3/4 mug **olive oil**

1. Mix everything but the oil together. Using the blender, gradually add the oil. Keep whisking and the dressing should turn thick and creamy.
2. Season with salt and pepper.

French dressing

1 teaspoon **sugar**
1 teaspoon **chives**
juice of 1 **lemon**
2 tablespoons **olive oil**
salt and **pepper**

1. Mix together, shake if possible.

Honey and lemon dressing

juice of one **lemon**
2 tablespoons **honey**
1 tablespoon **olive oil**
salt and **pepper**

1. Mix together, shake if possible.

Piquant dressing

3 tablespoons **olive oil**
2 tablespoons **white wine vinegar**
1 teaspoon **chopped chives**
1 teaspoon **paprika**
1 tablespoon **soy sauce**
1/4 teaspoon **wholegrain mustard**
3 tablespoons **water**
2 tablespoons **brown sugar**
salt and **pepper**

1. Mix all ingredients together.

Yogurt dressing

4 tablespoons **natural yogurt**
1/2 teaspoon **honey**
grated rind and juice of a **lemon**
2 **spring onions**, finely chopped
salt and **pepper**

1. Mix everything together.

Raspberry and balsamic dressing

1/3 x 400g pack of **frozen raspberries**, defrosted
4 tablespoons **balsamic vinegar**
4 tablespoons **olive oil**
1 tablespoon **sugar**

1. Push the defrosted raspberries through a sieve.
2. Mix together with the rest of the ingredients.

salad dressings **37**

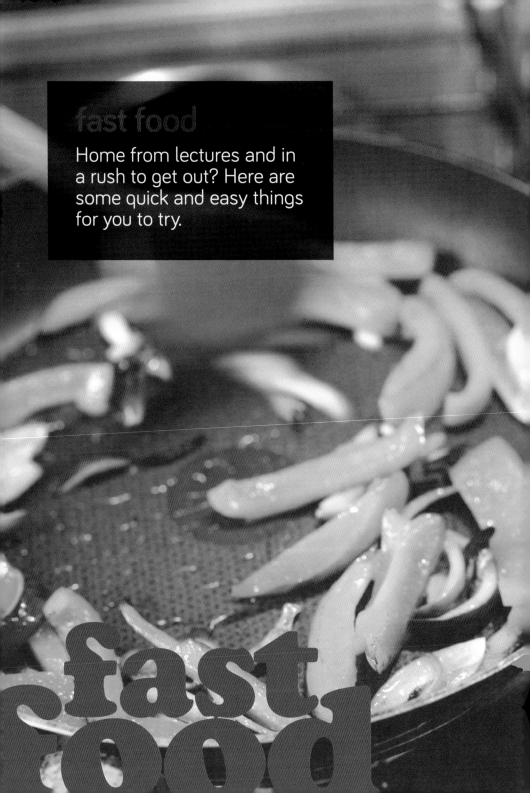

fast food

Home from lectures and in a rush to get out? Here are some quick and easy things for you to try.

fast
food

Chickpea and Feta Salad

£0.79 /PERSON

1

2

PREP 10 MINS

If you want to save half for the next day, divide into 2 portions before adding the dressing, as it causes the greens to wilt.

Croutons

1 tablespoon **oil** to fry

1 slice **white bread**

handful of fresh **spinach**

1/2 x 400g tin **chickpeas**, rinsed and drained

1/2 x 200g pack of **feta cheese**, cut into chunks

1 **red pepper**, roughly chopped

Choose a **dressing** from page 36. Make enough for 2.

1. Prepare a salad dressing. Alternatively, you can use a ready-made French dressing.

2. Make the croutons: heat oil in a frying pan and fry the bread on both sides. Cut into small squares.

3. Remove any large stalks from the spinach. Put in a bowl with the rest of the ingredients. Mix and add the dressing.

Sweet Potato and Pecan Salad

You can buy portions of celeriac in most supermarkets. Use any leftovers in casseroles, or roast with other vegetables

2 **sweet potatoes**, peeled and diced

French dressing (page 36)

4 **spring onions**, sliced

1 **celery** stick, sliced

½ mug grated **celeriac**

1 teaspoon **chives**

⅓ mug **pecan nuts**

a few **lettuce** leaves

£1.03 /PERSON

2

2

PREP 15 MINS

1. Peel and dice the sweet potato. Place in a pan of boiling water and simmer for 6 minutes until tender. Drain and set aside to cool.
2. Make the French dressing.
3. When the sweet potato has cooled, mix in the onions, celery, grated celeriac, chives and pecans.
4. Put the lettuce on a plate and pile the salad on top. Drizzle over the French dressing. Eat straight away.

Pineapple and Cashew Nut Salad

If you want to save half for the next day, remember to divide into 2 before adding the dressing.

1 portion of **rice** (see page 22)

6 florets of **broccoli**

1/2 x 160g pack of **sugar snaps**

1 small tin of **pineapple**, drained

1/2 mug **cashew nuts**

1/4 mug **raisins**

2 teaspoons **oil** to fry

Coconut dressing (page 36)

£1.15 /PERSON

2

2

PREP 25 MINS

1. Cook the rice (see page 22).

2. Add the broccoli to a pan of boiling water, simmer for 4 minutes and add the sugar snaps. Simmer for another 2 minutes and drain.

3. Chop the pineapple into bite-sized pieces.

4. Gently fry the cashew nuts, without oil, until golden brown.

5. Add all the ingredients together and pour over the coconut dressing.

Ciabatta Goat's Cheese Salad

Goat's cheese is a little more expensive than most cheeses, but has such a unique taste. Combined with ciabatta, it's a winner!

2 tablespoons **olive oil**

1 teaspoon vegetarian **green pesto**

½ teaspoon **white wine vinegar**

½ **ciabatta** loaf, save the other half

3 small **tomatoes**, sliced

125g pack of **goat's cheese**, sliced into 6

lettuce

£ 1.47 /PERSON

1

2

PREP 15 MINS

1. Preheat the oven to 220°C fan oven/240°C/Gas 9.

2. Mix together the oil, pesto and wine vinegar. Slice the ciabatta horizontally. Sprinkle some of the oil and vinegar over and place the sliced tomatoes on top.

3. Add the goat's cheese and brush with dressing. Place in the oven for 6 minutes.

4. Pour the remaining dressing over the lettuce and serve together.

Green Pesto Pasta with Broccoli

This is a good all-in-one meal. Pasta, broccoli and pine nuts provide a nice balanced meal. It is also quick and easy to make.

1 portion of **pasta** (conchiglie is shown in the photo)

½ a head of **broccoli**, broken into small 'trees'

1 dessertspoon **olive oil**

2 tablespoons **vegetarian green pesto**

1 tablespoon **pine nuts**

grated **Parmesan-style cheese**

£1.37 /PERSON

1

1

PREP 15 MINS

1. Cook the pasta (see page 23).
2. When the pasta has 5 minutes left to cook, add the broccoli to the saucepan. Once cooked, drain and return to the pan.
3. Combine the pesto, oil and pine nuts. Add to the pasta and broccoli.
4. Sprinkle the Parmesan over the top and serve.

Cannellini Bean Spaghetti

Very easy, very tasty and very quick. If you freeze half the sauce and beans, you will have a ready-made meal for another day.

2 portions of **spaghetti**
(see page 23)

1 tablespoon **oil** to fry

1 clove **garlic**, chopped

2 **mushrooms**, sliced

400g can **chopped tomatoes**

¼ mug **water**

½ teaspoon **sugar**

1 teaspoon **oregano**

½ x 310g can **cannellini beans**, rinsed and drained

12–15 **black olives**

£0.54
/PERSON

1

2

PREP
15 MINS

1. Put the spaghetti on to cook (see page 23). Once cooked, drain.

2. Heat the oil in a frying pan. Fry the garlic for 30 seconds, add the mushrooms and cook for 1 minute.

3. Add the rest of the ingredients and simmer for 4–5 minutes. Stir continuously.

4. Mix with the pasta and serve.

Roast Cherry Tomatoes and Spaghetti

Use any leftover feta in a salad or sandwich.

£1.32 /PERSON

8 **cherry tomatoes**

1 tablespoon **oil** to roast

1 portion of **spaghetti** (see page 23)

12–15 **olives**

⅓ x 200g block of **feta cheese**, cut into chunks

1 teaspoon **chives**

grated **Parmesan-style cheese** (optional)

1. Preheat the oven to 180°C fan oven/200°C/Gas 6.

2. Put the tomatoes in an ovenproof dish and drizzle with olive oil. Season with salt and pepper. Place in the oven for 15 minutes.

3. In the meantime, put the spaghetti on to cook (see page 23).

4. Drain the spaghetti and return to the pan with the olives, feta cheese and chives. When the tomatoes are cooked, tip them and the juices from the bottom of the dish into the pan. Mix together.

PREP 5 MINS

COOK 15 MINS

Goats Cheese Pancakes

£1.45 /PERSON

2

2

PREP 25 MINS

Onion Chutney

2 tablespoons **oil**

2 **onions**, sliced

1 teaspoon **flour**

1/2 **veg stock cube**

1/4 mug **water**

1 tablespoon **white wine vinegar**

1 teaspoon **honey**

12 **cherry tomatoes**

4 **eggs**

1 mug **self-raising flour**

pinch **salt**

1/4 teaspoon **paprika**

1/4 mug of **milk**

Flora to fry

150g **goats cheese**, cut into 8 slices

1. Heat the oil in a large saucepan. Add the onions and fry on a medium heat, stirring frequently, until the onions are browned and soft. Stir in the flour. Add the rest of the chutney ingredients and bring to the boil.

2. Beat together the eggs, flour, salt, paprika and milk in a bowl.

3. Heat a little Flora in a frying pan. Add tablespoons of the batter in the frying pan, it should make about 8. Allow them to cook on a medium heat for 1–2 minutes on one side.

4. Press a piece of goats cheese into each pancake.

5. Turn over and cook until both sides are browned.

6. Serve with the chutney

Tagliatelle with Red Pesto

You can add different vegetables to the sauce, such as green beans, mangetout, sugar snaps, etc.

1 portion of **tagliatelle** (see page 23)

1 tablespoon **oil** to fry

½ **onion**, chopped

½ **red pepper**, cut into chunks

2 **mushrooms**, sliced

1 **tomato**, cut into chunks

½ x 190g jar **vegetarian red pesto**

2 tablespoons **cream**

2 tablespoons **pine nuts**

grated **cheese** to serve

£2.28 /PERSON

2

1

PREP 20 MINS

1. Cook the tagliatelle (see page 23).

2. Fry the onion, pepper and mushroom for 2 minutes. Add the tomato and cook for 1 minute.

3. Add the pesto, cream and pine nuts and heat through.

4. Drain the tagliatelle and mix with the sauce. Finish with grated cheese.

Spinach and Cheese Rice Slice

This is a bit like quiche, without the bother of pastry. It is good either hot or cold, therefore it is ideal to make on one day and eat the rest the next day.

½ mug **basmati rice**

1 tablespoon **oil** to fry

1 small **red onion**, chopped

100g packet **fresh spinach**

1 mug Cheddar **cheese**

2 tablespoons **cream**

2 **eggs**, beaten

1 **tomato**, sliced

½ mug grated **cheese** for the top

£1.57 /PERSON

2

2

PREP 15 MINS

COOK 25 MINS

1. Preheat the oven to 180°C fan oven/200°C/Gas 6. Grease a small casserole dish.

2. Cook the rice (see page 22).

3. Heat the oil in a frying pan and fry the onions. Once they begin to soften, add the spinach and cook for 30 seconds. It will begin to wilt. Take off the heat.

4. Add the cooked rice, cheese, cream and beaten eggs. Season well and stir.

5. Pour into the casserole dish. Arrange the sliced tomatoes on the top. Sprinkle the grated cheese evenly over the top.

6. Cook in the oven for 25 minutes. The cheese should be brown.

Mexican Eggs

This is a good way to use up any leftover tortillas and makes a spicy breakfast alternative, or an interesting snack.

1 **corn tortilla**

1 tablespoon **oil** to fry

2 **spring onions**, chopped

1 small clove of **garlic**, chopped

½ **fat red chilli**, chopped

1 **tomato**, cut into chunks

3 **eggs**, beaten

1 teaspoon **chives**

£0.89 /PERSON

2

1

PREP 15 MINS

1. Cut the tortilla into strips and fry in oil until golden brown. Set aside.

2. Add the onions, garlic and chilli. Fry for 1 minute.
Add the tomatoes and fry for another minute.

3. Add the beaten eggs and chives and stir. Do not overcook the eggs; they need to be quite soft. Season with salt and pepper.

4. Put the tortilla strips on the plate together with the egg mixture.

Potato Pan Cake

1 large **potato**, diced

1 small **carrot**, chopped

a few florets of **broccoli**

1 tablespoon **oil** to fry

1 small **onion**, chopped

1 clove **garlic**, chopped

2 **tomatoes**, cut into chunks

½ x 200g pack of **feta cheese** or ½ x 390g **pack tofu**

£ 0.57 /PERSON

3

2

PREP 25 MINS

1. Put the potatoes and the carrots in a pan of boiling water, simmer for 5 minutes, then add the broccoli. Cook for a further 5 minutes until everything is tender.

2. Preheat the grill.

3. Heat the oil in a frying pan and fry the onions, garlic and tomatoes. Allow them to brown a little. Add the drained potatoes, broccoli and carrots. Fry together for 2–3 minutes. Stir in the tofu, or the feta cheese, and season with salt and pepper.

4. Place under the hot grill until the cheese browns. Be careful not to push the pan too far in, or the handle will burn.

Quick Veggie Pasta

1 tablespoon **oil** to fry
1 small **onion**, sliced
1 clove **garlic**, finely chopped
1 small **courgette**, sliced
4 **mushrooms**, sliced
10 **olives**, roughly chopped
4 **cherry tomatoes**, halved

Dressing

2 tablespoons **balsamic vinegar**
2 tablespoons **olive oil**
2 teaspoons **sugar**
salt and **pepper**

tagliatelle (see page 23)
Parmesan-style cheese to serve

£0.79 /PERSON

1

2

PREP 20 MINS

1. Put the pasta on to cook (see page 23).
2. Mix together the dressing ingredients. Set to one side.
3. Heat the oil in a wok. Add the onions, garlic and courgettes and fry until they begin to brown.
4. Add the mushrooms and fry for 1–2 minutes. Season well.
5. Add the olives and tomatoes and take off the heat. There will be enough heat in the pan to warm them.
6. Add the drained pasta. Stir.
7. Serve in bowls and drizzle with the dressing and grated Parmesan.

Feta Salad Wrap

Use the leftover feta in sandwiches (see page 26), or another salad.

see page 26

2-3 **corn tortilla wraps**

2-3 dessertspoons **crème fraîche**

½ **little gem lettuce**, sliced

1 **tomato**, sliced

7cm piece of **cucumber**, cut into long strips

2 **spring onions**, cut lengthways into strips

10 **stuffed green olives**

½ x 200g pack of **feta cheese**, crumbled

£0.92 /PERSON

1

2

PREP 15 MINS

1. Spread a dessertspoon of crème fraîche on each tortilla.

2. Divide the lettuce, tomato, cucumber, spring onions and olives between the tortillas.

3. Divide the feta cheese between the wraps. Season well.

Thai Coconut Curry

Good to heat up next day.

1 **carrot**, cut into bite-sized chunks

1 **sweet potato**, cut into 2cm cubes

1 **potato**, cut into 2cm cubes

½ x 200g pack **green beans**, each cut in half

1 small head **broccoli**, broken into small trees'

1 tablespoon **oil** to fry

1 **onion**, sliced

½ **red pepper**, cut into chunks

1 tablespoon **Thai red curry paste**

400ml tin **coconut milk**

basmati rice to serve (see page 22)

£0.72 /PERSON

1

4

PREP 30MINS

1. Add the carrot, sweet potato and potato to a pan of boiling water. Simmer for 5 minutes. Add the broccoli and beans and simmer for a further 5 minutes. Drain and return to the pan until needed.

2. Heat the oil in a wok and fry the onions and the peppers until they become soft.

3. Add the curry paste and fry for 30 seconds.

4. Add the coconut milk and vegetables and simmer for 5 minutes.

5. Serve with the rice (see page 22).

broke but hungry

Waiting for pay day, or is the loan rapidly running out? Here are some inexpensive dishes to keep the hunger pangs at bay.

French Onion Soup

You can use these cheesy croutons with other soups, experiment and enjoy.

1½ tablespoons **oil** to fry

1 large **onion**, sliced

1½ mugs **water** + 1 **vegetable stock** cube

½ teaspoon **Marmite**

Cheesy Croutons

1 slice **wholemeal bread**

¼ mug grated **cheese**

£0.50 /PERSON

2

2

PREP 20 MINS

COOK 10 MINS

1. Heat the oil in a saucepan. Add the sliced onions. Fry on a medium heat for 6–8 minutes until the onions are really brown, but not burned. You will need to watch them carefully and stir frequently.

2. Once the onions are really brown, add the water, crumbled stock cube and Marmite. Bring to the boil and then turn down to simmer for 5 minutes.

3. While the soup is cooking, make some cheese on toast (see page 28). You will not need to butter the toast. Once toasted, cut into squares to use as croutons.

4. Taste the soup and season. Pour into a bowl and drop the croutons on top.

Tomato and Lentil Soup

Use a hand-held blender for this recipe. If you don't have one, don't worry. It tastes just the same unblended. Make enough for 2 and eat the rest the next day.

1 tablespoon **oil** to fry

1 medium **onion**, chopped

1 medium **carrot**, chopped

1 clove **garlic**, chopped

¼ mug **red lentils**

400g can **tomatoes**

½ teaspoon **Marmite**

2 mugs **water** + 1 **vegetable stock cube**, crumbled in

bread to serve

£0.43 /PERSON

2

2

PREP 15 MINS

COOK 20 MINS

1. Heat the oil in a saucepan and add the onion, carrot and garlic. Cook until the onion is soft.

2. Add the lentils, tomatoes, Marmite, stock cube and water. Bring to the boil, then turn down and simmer for 20 minutes until the lentils are tender.

3. Once the soup is cooked, season well with salt and freshly ground black pepper. Use a hand-held blender to blitz the soup. Serve with bread.

Apple and Cashew Soup

£0.58 /PERSON

2

2

PREP 10 MINS

COOK 20 MINS

This soup is quick and easy to make. Make enough for 2 and you can keep the rest for the next day. Alternatively, freeze it and keep for a day when you are too busy to cook.

1 tablespoon **oil** to fry

2 **carrots**, sliced

1 small **onion**, chopped

1 small **potato**, cut into chunks

1 **eating apple**, cut into chunks

2 mugs **water**

1 **vegetable stock cube**, crumbled

½ x 100g pack of **cashews**, chopped

1. Heat the oil in a saucepan and fry the carrots, onion, potatoes and apple. Allow the vegetables to brown a little.

2. Add the rest of the ingredients and bring to the boil. Season with salt and pepper and simmer for 20 minutes until the vegetables are tender.

3. Whizz with the hand-held blender.

Sweetcorn Soup

Use the rest of the tin of sweetcorn in a risotto or salad.

1 tablespoon **oil** to fry
½ onion, sliced
1 **pepper**, red or green, cut into strips
1 mug of **water**

1 **vegetable stock cube**, crumbled
½ x 340g can of **sweetcorn**, drained
1 tablespoon **double cream**

£0.52 /PERSON

2

2

PREP 20 MINS

1. Heat the oil in a saucepan and fry the onion and pepper until the onion is soft.

2. Add the water and stock cube and bring to the boil. Add the sweetcorn and simmer for 3–4 minutes.

3. Whizz the soup with the blender, but do not make it too fine; keep it a bit lumpy. Stir in the cream and season with salt and pepper.

Lentil and Apricot Soup

Ready-to-eat dried apricots are usually found in the 'baking section' at the supermarket and make great, healthy snacks.

3 tablespoons **red lentils**

1 tablespoon chopped ready-to-eat **dried apricots**

1 medium **potato**, diced

juice of half a **lemon**

2 mugs **water** + 2 **vegetable stock cubes**, crumbled in

1 teaspoon **curry paste**

1 teaspoon **oregano**

---

1. Put all the ingredients in a saucepan. Bring to the boil, then turn down the heat and simmer for 30 minutes.

2. Whizz with the hand-held blender. Season well. Reheat and serve.

£0.39 /PERSON

1

2

PREP 10 MINS

COOK 30 MINS

Apple and Bean Salad

You can use any variety of canned beans. Always be sure to rinse them well, as some of the soaking juices are not good for you.

1 medium **potato** diced

1 **red dessert apple**

400g can of **borlotti beans**

2 **spring onions**, chopped

1 small **yellow pepper**, diced

Dressing

juice of a **lemon**

2 tablespoons **olive oil**

1 dessertspoon **wholegrain mustard**

1 teaspoon **sugar**

1 teaspoon **chives**

salt and **pepper**

£0.76 /PERSON

2

2

PREP 20 MINS

1. Put the diced potatoes in a pan of boiling water and simmer for 8 minutes. Drain.
2. Peel the apple, remove the core and chop into chunks.
3. Mix together the beans, apple, spring onions and pepper.
4. Mix together the dressing ingredients and mix with the salad.
5. Serve with green salad.

Potato Hash

So quick and easy. This is a good way to liven-up a potato and half a tin of beans.

2 medium **potatoes, diced**
½ x 400g tin **baked beans**

1 tablespoon **oil** to fry
½ mug grated **Cheddar cheese**

£ 0.71 /PERSON

2

1

PREP 25 MINS

1. Put the potatoes in a pan of boiling water and simmer for 8 minutes. Drain, return to the pan and squash them a little with a fork. Do not mash them.

2. Stir in the beans.

3. Heat some oil in a frying pan and tip the mixture in. Don't stir, allow it to fry and brown on the bottom. Once browned, using a slotted turner, stir all the browned bits up from the bottom, leave again to allow the rest to brown. Stir in the browned bits again.

4. Serve on a plate and put the grated cheese on the top, whilst it is still hot, so that it melts. Add some ketchup or HP.

Channa Dhal

This dish makes a meal in itself, or can be eaten with bread, naan bread, rice, or jacket potatoes. Use up any leftover coconut milk in a salad dressing or sauce (see pages 36 or 33).

1 tablespoon **oil** to fry

1 small **onion**, finely chopped

2 **cloves garlic**, finely chopped

½ teaspoon freshly grated **ginger**

1 tablespoon **curry paste**

½ x 400g can **tomatoes**

2 tablespoons **coconut milk**

400g tin of **chickpeas**

£0.52 /PERSON

1

2-3

PREP 15 MINS

1. Heat the oil in a frying pan and fry the onions and garlic until they begin to brown. Stir frequently. Once brown, add the ginger and curry paste. Cook for 1 minute.

2. Add the tomatoes, coconut milk and chickpeas. Season well with salt and pepper. Cook for about 5 minutes until the mixture begins to thicken.

Bean Burgers

If you want to keep one of the burgers for the next day, don't fry it, but wrap it in cling film and keep it in the fridge.

½ x 750g pack of frozen **broad beans,** defrosted

1 **egg**, beaten

1 slice **bread**, made into breadcrumbs

1 small **onion**, grated

1 bag **ready-salted crisps**, crushed

1 tablespoon **oil** to fry

Toppings

1 **onion**, sliced

pickles, e.g. gherkins

tomato sauce

£0.67 /PERSON

3

2-3

PREP 30 MINS

1. Mash the beans with a fork, or whizz with a blender. Don't make them too pulpy, leave a bit of texture.

2. Put the egg and breadcrumbs in a bowl and allow the bread to soak up the egg. Add the beans and mix.

3. Grate the onions and squeeze out most of the liquid. Add to the bean mixture and mix well.

4. Shape the mixture into 2-3 burgers. Put the crushed crisps on a plate and roll the burgers in them.

5. Heat oil in a frying pan and cook the burgers for about 5 minutes each side on a medium heat. Take care that they do not burn. If they begin to brown before the 5 minutes, turn down the heat.

6. While they are cooking, prepare the toppings. Heat a little oil in a saucepan and fry the onions on a medium heat until caramelised (i.e. really brown). You will need to stir them frequently.

7. Slice the burger bun in half, horizontally. Put the burger inside, with the onions on top and some tomato sauce and pickle to finish. Enjoy!

Greek Style Egg Curry

This recipe is quite spicy. You can vary the type and amount of curry paste you use. Stirring in the yogurt makes the curry milder.

1 tablespoon **oil** to fry

1 medium **onion**, sliced

½ can of **chopped tomatoes**

½ mug **frozen peas**

1 dessertspoon **curry paste**

4 **eggs**

2 tablespoons **Greek yogurt**

to serve

rice (see page 22)

mango chutney

£0.74 /PERSON

★3

2

PREP 25 MINS

1. Heat the oil in a frying pan, add the onion and cook on medium heat for 5 minutes until it begins to go brown. Stir frequently. Add the tomatoes, peas and curry paste. Bring to the boil, then simmer gently for 5 minutes.

2. Put the rice on to cook (see page 22).

3. Meanwhile, put the eggs on to boil for 8 minutes. When cooked, run cold water over them and then peel. Cut each egg in half.

4. Add the yogurt to the curry and mix.

5. Serve with rice, eggs and mango chutney.

Halloumi Rosti

2 medium **potatoes**, grated

125g **halloumi**, grated

2 **spring onions**, chopped

2 **sundried tomatoes**, chopped

½ **fat red chilli**, chopped

oil

2 **eggs**

£0.86 /PERSON

1

2

PREP 20 MINS

1. Squeeze the liquid out of the grated potatoes. Mix together the potatoes, halloumi, onions, tomatoes and chilli.

2. Heat the oil in a large frying pan and place the rosti mix in two piles in the pan. Spread out a little and press down to form two rosti.

3. Fry on a medium heat, turn over after 5 minutes. Fry until browned on both sides and cooked through.

4. Fry the eggs and serve one on top of each rosti.

Baked Patties with Chilli Sauce

Baking in the oven gives a 'roasted' flavour. If you have a little cream handy, make the spicy sauce to go with them. If not, make one of the sauces on pages 32 & 33.

£0.96 /PERSON

3

2

PREP 15 MINS

COOK 25 MINS

1 medium **potato**, diced

½ **onion**, grated

1 small **carrot**, grated

¼ mug grated **Parmesan-style cheese**

1 **courgette**, grated

1 stick **celery**, finely chopped

½ teaspoon **oregano**

1 **vegetable stock cube**, crumbled

1 beaten **egg**

Chilli sauce

½ mug **yoghurt**

2 tablespoons **mayo**

½ **fat red chilli**, chopped

salt and **pepper**

1. Preheat the oven to 180°C fan oven/200°C/Gas 6.

2. Put the potatoes in boiling water and simmer for 10 minutes. Drain and mash with a fork. Add the onion, carrot, cheese, courgette, celery, oregano, and stock cube. Season and mix. Add the egg a little at a time, taking care that the mixture does not get too soft. You will probably only need half the egg.

3. Grease a baking tray and pile the mixture into 3–4 piles. Shape into rounds. Cook in the oven for 25 minutes; the patties should go slightly brown.

4. To make the sauce, simply mix the ingredients.

Quorn Madras Curry

It's quite a good idea to keep a packet of Quorn in your freezer drawer.

1 tablespoon **oil** to fry

½ x 350g packet of **Quorn chicken-style** pieces

1 small **onion**, chopped

1 small **sweet potato**, peeled and cut into small chunks

1 **clove garlic,** chopped

1 tablespoon **Madras curry paste**

400g tin **chopped tomatoes**

1 mug **water** + 1 **vegetable stock cube**, crumbled

3 tablespoons **raisins**

rice to serve (see page 22)

£1.04 /PERSON

1

2-3

PREP 35 MINS

1. Heat the oil in a wok and fry the Quorn, onions, sweet potatoes and garlic until they all begin to brown.

2. Add the curry paste to the pan and cook for 30 seconds.

3. Add the rest of the ingredients. Simmer gently for 15–20 minutes.

4. Serve with rice (see page 22).

one-pot dishes

Tired of washing up loads of pots and pans? These one-pot dishes will minimise the clearing-up process.

one
pot
dishes

Biryani with Yogurt and Cashews

Try not to stir too much in stage 3 as the rice will become mushy.

50g **butter**, measure by packet

1 medium **onion**, cut into wedges

2 tablespoons **Korma curry paste**

1 mug **rice**

1 dessertspoon **liquid vegetable stock** or a stock cube

1 mug **Greek yogurt**

1 small **cauliflower**, cut into florets

1 mug **frozen peas**

½ mug **raisins**

100g pack **cashews**

1 teaspoon **turmeric**

2 mugs **water**

naan breads

£0.89 /PERSON

3

4

PREP 35 MINS

1. Heat the butter in a large pan, or wok, and cook the onions until they become soft. Add the Korma paste and turmeric and cook for 1 minute.

2. Add the rice and stir well. Cook for 1 minute, allowing the rice to absorb the flavours.

3. Add the stock, yogurt, cauliflower, peas, raisins, cashews and water. Bring to the boil. Turn down the heat to low and simmer with the lid on (you can use foil if the wok does not have a lid) for 25 minutes. Check every 10 minutes to make sure it is not sticking to the bottom. You may need to add a little more water. Serve with warm naan breads.

Sweet Potato Tagine

You could also eat this with rice, potatoes or crusty bread.

£0.86 /PERSON

3

4

PREP 30 MINS

2 tablespoons **oil** to fry

1 **onion**, chopped

2 cloves **garlic**, finely chopped

2 teaspoons ground **coriander**

2 teaspoons **cumin**

2 teaspoons **paprika**

1 small **aubergine**, cut into cubes

2 small **sweet potatoes**, peeled and cut into cubes

400g tin **chopped tomatoes**

1 mug **water**

6 ready-to-eat dried **apricots**, chopped

2 teaspoons **sugar**

1/2 mug **raisins**

400g tin **chickpeas**, washed and drained

1 **courgette**, cut into chunks

1 tablespoon **tomato purée**

1 mug of **couscous**

2 mugs **water** + 1 **vegetable stock cube**

1. Heat the oil in a wok or large saucepan. Add the onions and garlic and fry until the onions are soft.

2. Add the coriander, cumin and paprika and fry for 30 seconds.

3. Add the aubergines and the sweet potatoes to the wok and fry for 1 minute. Stir frequently.

4. Add the tin of tomatoes, water, apricots, sugar, raisins and chickpeas. Bring to the boil and then simmer gently, for 10 minutes. Cover with a lid or some foil.

5. Add the courgettes and the tomato purée and simmer for a further 5 minutes.

6. While the tagine is cooking, put the couscous in a bowl and add the boiling water and stock cube. Cover with a plate and leave to stand for 5 minutes until all the water is absorbed.

7. Serve the tagine on the couscous.

Fancy a bit more spice? Why not try Joy's Saffron Vegetable Tagine. You can find her recipe at noshbooks.com/saffron

Leek and Potato Frittata with Salad

Frittata is a good way to make a meal in one pan. You can add many different kinds of things, for example, tomatoes or mushrooms.

£0.67 /PERSON

4

4

PREP 30 MINS

1 large **potato,** cut into 2cm cubes

oil for roasting

50g **butter** to fry, measure by packet

2 small **leeks,** cut into slices

6 large **eggs,** beaten

200g block of **feta cheese,** cubed

2 teaspoons **dried basil**

½ mug grated **Cheddar cheese**

Piquant Tomato Sauce to serve (see page 32)

salad to serve

1. Preheat the oven to 200°C fan oven/220°C/Gas 7.
2. Put the cubed potatoes on a baking tray, sprinkle with oil. Season well and distribute the oil evenly with your hands. Place in the oven for 20 minutes until they are browned.
3. Preheat the grill.
4. Heat the butter in a frying pan and add the leeks. Cook until they are tender.
5. Beat the eggs in a bowl, then add to the frying pan. Cook for 1 minute or until the egg at the bottom of the pan begins to set. Gently move the egg around in the pan to allow the runny egg to get to the bottom of the pan.
6. Add the cooked potatoes, feta cheese and the basil. Sprinkle the Cheddar cheese over the top.
7. Place under the grill for 5–6 minutes until the cheese browns and the egg is set.
8. Serve with the tomato sauce.

We love fritattas. Not only are they easy and tasty, you also don't have much washing up to do. Try Joy's Spaghetti Fritatta at noshbooks.com/fritatta

Roast Sweet Potatoes with Couscous and Balsamic Dressing

Roasting vegetables is so easy and enhances the flavours. If you use other veggies, remember to cut small the ones which take the longest to cook (see page 21).

1 **sweet potato**, peeled and cut into small chunks

1 **red pepper**, cut into large chunks

1 **courgette**, cut into slices

1 **onion**, cut into wedges

2 cloves **garlic**, left whole

2 tablespoons **olive oil**

1 teaspoon **dried rosemary**

1/2 mug **couscous**

1 mug boiling **water + vegetable stock cube**

400g can **black-eyed beans**, drained and rinsed

Dressing

2 tablespoons **balsamic vinegar**

2 tablespoons **olive oil**

2 teaspoons **sugar**

salt and **pepper**

£1.23 /PERSON

1

2

PREP 15 MINS

COOK 25 MINS

1. Preheat the oven to 200°C fan oven/220°C/Gas 7.

2. Place the sweet potato, pepper, courgette, onion and garlic on a baking tray. Season well with salt and pepper. Sprinkle with the olive oil and mix everything together well to distribute the oil evenly. Sprinkle the rosemary over the top and place in the oven for 25 minutes, or until the veggies are browned.

3. While the veggies are in the oven, put the couscous in a bowl and pour over the boiling water and stir in the stock cube. Cover the bowl and leave until all the water is absorbed.

4. Mix together the dressing ingredients.

5. Simmer the beans in a little water for 1 minute and then drain.

6. Once the veggies are cooked, mix together with the beans. Drizzle over the dressing.

7. Serve with the couscous.

Korma Rice and Spinach

If you like your food spicy, add an extra tablespoon of curry paste or use a hotter paste like Madras. The recipe just uses a wok, so not too much washing up here.

£1.97 /PERSON

2

2

PREP 30 MINS

1 tablespoon **oil** to fry

1 **onion**, sliced

1 clove **garlic**, chopped finely

1 tablespoon **Korma curry paste**

2 **tomatoes**, chopped

½ mug basmati **rice**

1 mug **water** + 1 **vegetable stock cube**

½ x 400g tin **chickpeas**, washed and drained

½ mug **raisins**

½ x 100g pack **pine nuts**

½ x 200g pack of fresh **spinach**

crème fraîche or natural **yogurt** to serve

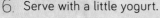

1. Heat a little oil in a wok. Add the onions and garlic and fry until soft.

2. Add the curry paste and tomatoes and fry for 30 seconds. Add the uncooked rice and cook for a further 30 seconds.

3. Add the stock and water and bring to the boil.

4. Add the chickpeas and the raisins. Turn down to simmer for 10–15 minutes until most of the water has been absorbed.

5. Add the pine nuts and the fresh spinach. Stir until the spinach is wilted. Should only take 30 seconds or so.

6. Serve with a little yogurt.

Leek and Potato Gratin

2 medium **potatoes**, cut into 2 cm chunks

2cm cube **butter**

1 tablespoon **oil**

2 **leeks**, sliced

100g **mushrooms** quartered

1 mug defrosted **frozen peas**

½ mug **double cream**

½ mug grated **Gruyère cheese** (can use **Cheddar**)

£1.64 /PERSON

2

2

PREP 15 MINS

COOK 25 MINS

1. Preheat the oven to 180ºC fan oven/200ºC/gas 6.

2. Put the potatoes in a pan of boiling water and simmer for 10 minutes. Drain and return to the pan. Add the butter and mix. Set to one side.

3. Meanwhile heat the oil in a frying pan and add the leeks. Fry until they begin to soften.

4. Add the mushrooms and fry for 1 minute.

5. Add the peas and cream and bring to the boil. Transfer to a small casserole dish. Pile the potatoes over the top and sprinkle the cheese over.

6. Bake in the oven for 25 minutes, the top should be golden brown.

Basic Risotto

Risotto is a very versatile recipe. The instructions below give you the basic idea and then you can experiment and add different ingredients yourself. Arborio rice is the best to use for risotto, but you can use long grain or other varieties.

1 tablespoon **oil** to fry
½ **onion**, chopped
1 clove of **garlic**, chopped
½ mug **Arborio/risotto rice**
1½ mugs **water**
1 **vegetable stock cube**

1 **leek**, sliced
½ **courgette**, cut into small pieces.
2 **mushrooms**, sliced
1 tablespoon **pine nuts**

£2.20 /PERSON

2

1

PREP 10 MINS

COOK 30 MINS

1. Heat the oil in a frying pan and fry the onions and garlic for 1 minute. Add the rice and fry for another minute.

2. Add the water, crumbled stock cube, leeks, courgette and mushrooms. Bring to the boil and season well with salt and pepper.

3. Simmer, with a lid on the pan (use foil if no lid), for 10-15 minutes until the rice is tender and the liquid is almost gone. Risotto should not be really dry. Don't allow all the liquid to boil away. Add more liquid if necessary.

4. Add the pine nuts at the end of the cooking time. Season well.

Variations on Risotto

Here are a few ideas for variations on the basic risotto recipe. If you are using v. which cook in a short time, they need to be added towards the end of the cooking time. Broccoli is not great in risotto, because it tends to break up and go mushy. These variations begin at stage 2 of the basic recipe. So, always begin with the onions, garlic and rice and water.

Green Veg Risotto

At stage 2, add green beans, cut into pieces, peas and broad beans.

At the end of the cooking time, add some spinach and cook until it wilts.

Serve topped with grated Parmesan-style cheese.

Spicy Pumpkin Risotto

At stage 2, add 1 small deseeded and chopped chilli, a vegetable stock cube, pieces of pumpkin or squash, half a courgette, chopped, and 2 sliced mushrooms.

At the end of the cooking time, top with grated Cheddar cheese; it will melt into the risotto. Don't try to cook the cheese or stir it in.

Green Pepper and Sweetcorn Risotto

At stage 2, add half a green pepper, roughly chopped and a sliced mushroom.

5 minutes before the end of the cooking time, add a small tin of sweetcorn and a tablespoon of cashew nuts.

Spicy Bean Risotto

At stage 2, add 1 tablespoon black-eyed beans, either tinned or soaked, 1 carrot, chopped, 1 small courgette, chopped, 2 teaspoons curry paste and some chives.

Mexican Risotto

At stage 2, replace 1 mug of water with $1/2$ a 400g tin of chopped tomatoes.

Also add, 1 chopped red pepper, 1 deseeded red chilli, chopped, half a tin of chickpeas and a teaspoon of sugar.

Serve topped with grated Cheddar cheese, or with soured cream.

Spanish Risotto

At stage 2, replace the 1 mug of water with $1/2$ a 400g tin of chopped tomatoes.

Also, add 2 sliced mushrooms and $1/2$ a chopped, red pepper.

5 minutes before the end, add 6–8 olives.

Serve topped with a fried egg.

y

f a staple dish for vegetarian students. Here is a basic
riations for you to work on. If you want to use root
carrots, parsnips, swedes, etc.), you will need to precook
Pictured opposite is Ginger and Corn Stir-fry.

£1.59 /PERSON

2

1

PREP 25 MINS

y
ed

1 teaspoon freshly grated **ginger**

2 **spring onions**, chopped

6 pieces **baby sweetcorn**, cut in half

1/2 red **pepper**, sliced

6 **sugar snaps** or **mangetout**

1/2 mug **water** with 1 **vegetable stock cube**, crumbled

2 tablespoons **soy sauce**

5cm piece of **courgette**, sliced

3 small florets of **broccoli**

1/2 x 200g pack of **ready-to-use noodles**

---

1. Heat the oil in a wok. If you do not have one, a frying pan is fine. Fry the garlic, ginger and onion for 1–2 minutes, then add the rest of the ingredients, apart from the noodles. Keep the heat high and cook for 4–5 minutes until the vegetables are cooked and almost all of the liquid has reduced. You can cover with a lid or some foil.

2. Stir in the noodles. Heat for 1 minute.

3. Season well with salt and pepper and eat straight away.

Stir-fry variations

Stir-frying is easy. To avoid overcooked vegetables, use only a small amount of water, stock, or sauce. Cut the vegetables up quite small: this looks better and cooks quicker. Cook the onions and garlic first, then add the other ingredients. Soy sauce, chilli sauce, hoisin sauce, etc., are great to use. Keep a few of these sauces in your storecupboard.

Tomato with vegetables

£0.52 /PERSON

1/2 **onion**, finely chopped

1 clove **garlic**, finely chopped

1 **courgette**, sliced

1/2 **pepper**, sliced

2 slices of **aubergine**

2 **mushrooms**, sliced

1 tablespoon **oil** to fry

1. Fry all the ingredients first in a little oil.
2. Add 1/2 tin of **chopped tomatoes,** and 1 teaspoon of **HP sauce.**
3. Cook for 3–4 minutes.
4. Add noodles.

Spinach

£0.51 /PERSON

2 **spring onions**, sliced

1 clove of **garlic,** finely chopped

1/2 **red pepper**, thinly sliced

1 teaspoon **soy sauce**

1 teaspoon **honey**

1/2 mug **water**

handful of **spinach**

2 tablespoons **pine nuts**

1. Fry the onions garlic and peppers.
2. Add the water, soy and honey and heat for 30 seconds.
3. Add the spinach and nuts and heat for 30 seconds.

Bean sprouts and vegetables

£0.87 /PERSON

2 **spring onions**, chopped

1 clove **garlic**, chopped

1 **pepper**, sliced

1 **courgette**, sliced

2 **mushrooms**, sliced

6 **sugar snaps**

1 teaspoon **soy sauce**

1 teaspoon **sugar**

1/2 mug **water**

handful of **bean sprouts**

1 tablespoon **pine nuts**

1. Fry the onions, garlic, peppers and courgettes for 2–3 minutes.
2. Add the mushrooms, sugar snaps, water, soy and sugar. Cook for 1 minute.
3. Add the bean sprouts and pine nuts and cook for 30 seconds.

Creamy vegetables

1 tablespoon **oil** to fry

1 small **onion**, chopped

1 **carrot**, finely chopped

2 thin slices of **aubergine**

2 **mushrooms**, sliced

1/2 green **pepper**, sliced or chopped

1/2 **vegetable stock cube**, crumbled + 1/2 mug **water**

2 tablespoons **double cream**

1. Fry the onions, carrot and aubergine for 2–3 minutes.
2. Add the peppers and mushrooms. Cook for 1 minute.
3. Add the rest of the ingredients and cook until heated through.

Cashews and vegetables

firm **tofu** (1/4 pack)

1 teaspoon **hoisin sauce**

1 tablespoon **cashews**

1/2 **pepper**, chopped

1 clove **garlic**, chopped

2 **spring onions,** chopped

6–8 **sugar snaps**

1/2 **vegetable stock cube** (crumbled) + 1/2 mug **water**

handful of **bean sprouts**

1. Fry the onion, garlic and peppers for 2 minutes.
2. Add the sugar snaps, hoisin, water and stock, cook for 1 minute.
3. Add the bean sprouts and tofu and heat through.

Other things to use as sauces:

coconut milk mixed with a teaspoon of **curry paste**

chilli sauce

tomato sauce

vegetable stock

Other things to add to stir-fry:

egg noodles: a handful per person

rice noodles: a handful per person

rice: (see page 22)

omelette strips: to make these, beat an egg and, before you start cooking the vegetables, put a little oil in the pan, pour in the egg and spread it around the pan, just like a pancake. Cook until it is brown on one side, then turn it over. When cooked, take out of the pan and cut into strips. Add to the stir-fry at the end. Use 1 egg per person.

fried tortilla wraps: fry and cut into strips and add at the end to keep them crisp. Use 1 **tortilla** per person.

Spicy Chickpeas with Spinach

Chickpeas are high in protein and inexpensive. Good to reheat the next day. Serve with jacket potatoes, or rice, and yogurt.

£1.60 /PERSON

2

2

PREP 15 MINS

COOK 10 MINS

1 tablespoon **oil** to fry

½ **red onion**, chopped

2 **tomatoes**, chopped

1 dessertspoon **curry paste**

⅔ mug **water** + 1 **vegetable stock cube**

400g can **chickpeas**, drained and rinsed

¼ x 200g pack of **spinach**

1 mug grated **cheese**

yogurt to serve

1. Heat the oil in a saucepan and fry the onion until it becomes soft.

2. Add the tomatoes, curry paste, water, crumbled stock cube and chickpeas. Bring to the boil and then simmer for about 10 minutes.

3. Add the spinach and stir until it wilts, about 30 seconds.

4. Take off the heat and stir in the cheese, which will melt. Season with salt and pepper.

5. Serve with jacket potatoes (page 24), or rice (see page 22), and yogurt.

Quorn Chilli with Aduki Beans

This is good to reheat the next day. Aduki beans are a bit more tender than red kidney beans, but you can use either.

1 tablespoon **oil** to fry

1 **onion**, chopped

1 clove **garlic**, finely chopped

350g packet of **Quorn mince**

1 tin **aduki beans**

400g tin **tomatoes**

6 **mushrooms**, sliced

2 teaspoons **chilli powder**

2 tablespoons **tomato purée**

½ mug **water**

1 teaspoon **sugar**

rice (see page 22) or **bread** to serve

1. Heat the oil in a wok, or large saucepan, and fry the onions and garlic until the onions are soft.

2. Add the rest of the ingredients, bring to the boil, then turn down to simmer for 10–15 minutes.

3. Serve with crusty bread or rice (see page 22).

Squash and Apple Curry

Serve with yogurt, naan bread and rice. Use the rest of the butternut squash to make soup. Use the Leek Soup recipe on page 155, replacing the potato and carrot with the butternut squash.

1 tablespoon **oil** to fry

1 small **onion**, chopped

2 large **potatoes**, diced

½ **butternut squash**, peeled and cut into small chunks

1 eating **apple**, cored and chopped into chunks

1 mug **water**

1 **vegetable stock cube**

1 tablespoon **raisins**

1 teaspoon **curry paste**

naan bread, **rice** (see page 22) and **yogurt** to serve

£0.84 /PERSON

1

2

PREP 30 MINS

COOK 20 MINS

1. Heat the oil in a saucepan. Add the onions, potatoes and squash and fry for 5 minutes until they begin to brown.

2. Add the apple, water, crumbled stock cube, raisins and curry paste. Bring to the boil. Turn down the heat, put the lid on the pan and simmer for 15–20 minutes until the vegetables are cooked.

Aubergine and Coconut Curry

You can add other vegetables to this recipe, just remember to allow enough simmering time for the vegetables to cook. Use the timings on page 20 as a guide.

1 tablespoon **oil** to fry

1 **onion**, sliced

1 clove **garlic**, chopped

1 tablespoon **curry paste**

1 **aubergine**, sliced

400ml can **coconut milk**

½ mug defrosted **frozen peas**

rice (see page 22)

yogurt to serve

£1.40 /PERSON

2

2

PREP 15 MINS

COOK 15 MINS

1. Fry the onions and garlic in a saucepan. When the onions begin to brown, add the curry paste and coconut milk.

2. Bring to the boil and then add the aubergines.

3. Simmer for 10 minutes until the aubergine is soft and then add the peas.

4. Serve with rice (see page 22) and yogurt.

something mum might cook

Missing home and never thought you would? Here are a few ideas to remind you of your mum's cooking.

Pasta with Roast Vegetables

Roasting vegetables is so easy and creates a delicious flavour as the starches in the vegetables caramelise (see page 21 for roasting other vegetables).

½ **onion**, cut into wedges

1 **sweet potato**, cut into 2 cm chunks

1 clove **garlic**, chopped

1 tablespoon **oil** to roast

6 **cherry tomatoes**

2 **mushrooms**, sliced

400g tin cannellini beans, washed and drained

1 portion of **pasta** (see page 23)

£0.61 /PERSON

2

2

PREP 15 MINS

COOK 30 MINS

1. Preheat the oven to 200°C fan oven/240°C/Gas 7.
2. Put the onion, courgette, chopped garlic, cherry tomatoes, mushrooms and beans on a baking tray. Sprinkle on the oil and season with salt and pepper. Toss the vegetables in the oil and seasoning so it is evenly distributed.
3. Roast in the oven for 25–30 minutes.
4. Cook the pasta (see page 23) 15 minutes from the end of the roasting time.
5. Drain the pasta and add the roasted veg, complete with all the juices. Mix and serve.

something mum might cook 89

Khitcherie

Here the split peas and nuts provide the protein, etc. It can be eaten on its own, or as a rice dish with other things. You can vary the amount of curry paste to your taste.

£1.07 /PERSON

3

2

PREP 30 MINS

½ mug **split peas**, soaked overnight

2 tablespoons **oil** to fry

½ **onion**, chopped

1 clove **garlic**, chopped

1 **fresh chilli**, chopped

1 teaspoon grated fresh **ginger**

1½ mugs **water**

½ mug **raisins**

1 dessertspoon **curry paste**

1 mug basmati **rice**

½ mug toasted **cashews**, roughly chopped

1. Put the split peas in a bowl and cover with cold water. Soak overnight.

2. Heat the oil in a saucepan and add the onions, garlic, chilli and ginger. Stir frequently and cook for 2–3 minutes.

3. Add the rice, drained split peas, water, raisins and curry paste. Bring to the boil, then turn down to simmer for 15 minutes, or until the rice is cooked. The liquid should have almost boiled away. If not, allow to cook a little more. Take off the heat and stir in the toasted cashews.

4. Serve with yogurt.

Bubble and Squeak

If you have any leftover veggies, they are ideal to use in this dish.

1 small **carrot**, chopped

1 medium **potato**, diced

1 small **sweet potato**, peeled and cut into chunks

½ mug frozen **peas**

1 mug shredded **cabbage**

1 tablespoon **oil** to fry

1 small **onion**, chopped

1 dessertspoon **chives**

½ mug **toasted cashews**, roughly chopped

½ mug grated **cheese**

Tomato Sauce (see page 33)

£ 0.96 /PERSON

2

2

PREP 30 MINS

1. Put the carrot in a pan of boiling water, simmer for 5 minutes, add the potato and sweet potato and simmer for another 7 minutes. Add the peas and cabbage and boil for a further 3 minutes. Drain the vegetables.

2. Turn the grill on to heat up.

3. Heat a little oil in a frying pan and fry the onions until they begin to brown. Add the drained vegetables and the chives. Fry for 2–3 minutes, stirring frequently. Season well.

4. Sprinkle the top with the grated cheese and the cashews. Place the frying pan under the grill until the cheese is browned.

5. Serve with the Tomato Sauce (see page 33).

No Pastry Quiche

You can add other vegetables to the basic recipe at the end of stage 2. Broccoli, squash, etc. will need to be precooked. Eat any leftovers, cold, the next day.

1 tablespoon **oil** to fry

1 **red onion**, cut into wedges

1 **courgette**, cut into chunks

1 **pepper**, cut into chunks

4-5 **cherry tomatoes**, cut in half

4 **eggs**, beaten

1/2 mug **milk**

3/4 mug grated **Parmesan-style cheese**

1 teaspoon dried **basil**

£1.10 /PERSON

2

2

PREP 20 MINS

COOK 25 MINS

1. Preheat the oven to 180°C fan oven/200°C/Gas 6.

2. Fry the onion, pepper and courgette in the oil for 3-4 minutes until they begin to brown. Transfer to a greased casserole dish. Add the tomatoes.

3. Beat the eggs in a bowl and add the milk, Parmesan and basil. Mix well. Season and pour over the vegetables. Cook in the oven for 20-25 minutes until the top begins to brown.

4. Serve either hot or cold, with salad or baked potatoes (see page 24).

Sweet Potato Patties

The yogurt dressing works well with the sweet potatoes, but you can choose other dressings from page 36 and serve with some of the salad recipes.

2 medium **sweet potatoes**, peeled and cut into chunks

1 tablespoon **oil** to fry

1 **leek**, chopped

1 clove **garlic**, chopped

1 teaspoon freshly grated **ginger**

2 tablespoons **sweetcorn**, drained

1 tablespoon **crème fraîche**

yogurt dressing (page 37)

salad

£0.93 /PERSON

3

2

PREP 15 MINS

COOK 25 MINS

1. Preheat the oven to 180°C fan oven/200°C/Gas 6.

2. Put the sweet potatoes in a pan of boiling water and simmer for 10 minutes. Drain and mash with a fork.

3. Heat a little oil in a frying pan and fry the leek, garlic and ginger for 2–3 minutes. Add the sweetcorn and take off the heat.

4. Add the potatoes and crème fraîche and season with salt and pepper. Mix together.

5. Grease a baking tray and spoon the mixture into 4 or 5 piles. Brush the top with a little oil. Cook in the oven for 25 minutes until they are a little brown on the top.

6. Serve with the yogurt dressing and some salad.

Nutty Crumble

You can vary the vegetables as you wish. If you use broccoli, or other vegetables that cook quickly, add towards the end of stage 2.

1 tablespoon **oil** to fry

1 **sweet potato** (you could use normal ones), peeled and chopped

1 **parsnip**, peeled and roughly chopped

1 **carrot**, peeled and chopped

1 **onion**, cut into wedges

1 mug **frozen peas**

400g tin **chopped tomatoes**

½ mug **water** + 1 **vegetable stock cube**

Crumble topping

¾ mug **plain flour**, or equal proportions of buckwheat and plain flour

50g block **butter** (measure using packet)

½ mug grated **Cheddar cheese**

½ mug **nuts**, chopped (use any variety, pine nuts, or cashews work well)

£1.54 /PERSON

3

2-3

PREP 20 MINS

COOK 30 MINS

---

1. Preheat the oven to 170°C fan oven/190°C/Gas 5.

2. Heat the oil in a saucepan and fry the sweet potato, parsnip, carrot and onion for 4-5 minutes. Stir frequently. Allow them to brown a little.

3. Add the frozen peas, tin of tomatoes, water and crumbled vegetable stock cube and bring to the boil. Turn down the heat and simmer for 10 minutes, or until they are tender.

4. While the vegetables are cooking, put the flour and butter in a bowl and rub in the butter using your finger ends and thumbs. The mixture should resemble breadcrumbs. Add the cheese and nuts. Mix together.

5. When the vegetables are cooked, pour into a casserole dish. Sprinkle the crumble mixture, evenly, over the top. Press down gently to compact the crumble.

6. Cook in the oven for 25-30 minutes.

Roast Tomato and Halloumi Salad

£1.36 /PERSON

2

2

PREP 35 MINS

COOK 25 MINS

3 **tomatoes**, cut into ¼'s

1 **red onion**, sliced

½ teaspoon **paprika**

1 tablespoon **oil**

½ mug **red Camargue rice**

½ x 400g tin **cannellini beans**, drained and rinsed

Dressing

1 tablespoon **oil**

juice of ½ **lemon**

1 dessertspoon **honey**

100g **halloumi**

1. Preheat the oven to 180ºC fan oven/200ºC/gas 6.

2. Put the tomatoes and onion on a roasting tray. Sprinkle the paprika over and season with salt and pepper. Drizzle over the oil and then mix everything together. Roast in the oven for 25 minutes.

3. Meanwhile put the rice in a pan of boiling water, simmer for 25–30 minutes, with a lid on the pan. Drain and return to the pan.

4. Add the beans to the roasting tray and return to the oven for a further 15 minutes. Take out of the oven, add the rice and pour over the dressing and mix everything together.

5. Heat the oil in a frying pan and add the sliced halloumi. Fry on a high heat until browned on both sides. Remove from the pan and cut into small chunks. Serve on top of the rice mix.

Corn Cakes & Ratatouille

These are best eaten straight away. You can keep the batter for making the corn cakes in the fridge for the next day, but no longer. Ratatouille is a versatile dish and goes well with bean burgers, vegetarian sausages, or any of the patty recipes in this book.

£1.32 /PERSON

3

2

PREP 25 MINS

Ratatouille

1 tablespoon **oil** to fry

½ **onion**, chopped

1 small clove **garlic**, chopped

1 **baby aubergine**, sliced

1 small **courgette**, sliced

1 **red** or **green pepper**, sliced

2 large **mushrooms**, sliced

400g tin **chopped tomatoes**

Corn Cakes

2/3 mug **self-raising flour**

1 **egg**

1/3 mug **milk**

130g can of **sweetcorn**, drained

1 tablespoon **oil** to fry

1. To make the ratatouille, heat the oil in a saucepan. Add the onions and garlic and cook for 3–4 minutes until the onions begin to brown. Add the other vegetables and allow them to fry a little. When they are beginning to cook, add the tin of tomatoes. Season. Bring to the boil and then turn down to simmer for 10 minutes.

2. To make the corn cakes, put the flour in a bowl. Make a well in the centre and add the egg and some of the milk. Beat with a wooden spoon. Add enough milk to make a thick, creamy consistency. Add the drained corn, this will make the batter a bit thinner.

3. Heat the oil in a frying pan. Drop 3 or 4 separate, heaped tablespoons of the batter mixture into the pan. Allow them to cook and become solid and browned underneath. Turn them over and allow them to brown on the other side. They should be cooked in the middle, but if not, turn down the heat and cook for a little longer.

4. Serve with the ratatouille.

Veggie Bake with Tomato Sauce

Veggie bake is another easy, basic recipe, which can be varied by using different vegetables and also different sauces. You can use the Tomato Sauce or Quick Cheese Sauce recipes on page 33. Always put the grated cheese on the top, to give a tasty crunch.

£1.09 /PERSON

2

2

PREP 20 MINS

COOK 30 MINS

1 **carrot**, diced

1 **potato**, diced

1 medium **sweet potato**, peeled and cut into chunks

4–5 **spring onions** or 1 **small onion**, chopped

1 tablespoon **oil** to fry

1 **courgette**, sliced

6 **cherry tomatoes,** halved

1 teaspoon **chives**

½ mug grated **cheese**

Tomato Sauce (see page 33)

bread to serve

1. Put the carrots, potatoes and sweet potatoes in a pan of boiling water and simmer for 10 minutes. Drain and return to the pan.

2. Preheat the oven to 180°C fan oven/200°C/Gas 6.

3. Fry the onions and courgettes. Once they begin to brown, take off the heat.

4. Add to the potato pan, together with the tomatoes, chives and tomato sauce. Mix together and then pour into a greased casserole dish. Top with grated cheese. Bake in the oven for 25–30 minutes until the cheese is browned.

5. Serve with crusty bread.

Honey Mushroom and Rice Pie

Ready-rolled pastry is really handy and easy to use. It adds a little more variety to your food.

1 mug **water**

½ mug **rice**

1 teaspoon **pilau rice seasoning**

1 tablespoon **oil** to fry

2 **onions**, sliced

100g pack **pine nuts**

250g pack **mushrooms**, sliced

2 teaspoons **fennel seeds**

2 teaspoons **honey**

375g pack ready-rolled **puff pastry**

1 beaten **egg**

£1.99 /PERSON

4

3-4

PREP 25 MINS

COOK 25 MINS

1. Preheat the oven to 200°C fan oven/220°C/Gas 7.

2. Put 1 mug of boiling water in a pan. Add the rice and pilau rice seasoning and simmer, with a lid on the pan, for 10–15 minutes.

3. Heat the oil in a pan and fry the onions until they become soft. Add the pine nuts and fry until they become slightly brown. Add the mushrooms and fry for 30 seconds. Add the fennel seeds and the honey. Season with salt and pepper.

4. Put half the onion and mushrooms on the bottom of a small casserole dish. Put the rice on top, with the rest of the onions and mushrooms on top of the rice.

5. Unroll the pastry and place on top of the pie. Cut to size and pinch the edges. Brush the top with beaten egg.

6. Place in the oven for 20–25 minutes until browned on top.

Carrot Pancakes, Hummus and Salad

The hummus will keep until the next day and is great eaten with some celery sticks.

£1.12 /PERSON

3

2-3

PREP 30 MINS

Hummus

400g tin **chickpeas**, rinsed and drained

4 **sun-dried tomatoes**, chopped

juice of a **lemon**

1 tablespoon **olive oil**

Pancakes

2 **eggs**

1/2 mug **self-raising flour**

1 teaspoon ground **cumin**

1 teaspoon ground **coriander**

1 small **onion**, grated

3 **carrots**, peeled and grated

oil to fry

Salad

1 little gem **lettuce**, cut horizontally

2 **spring onions**, cut into thin strips

7cm piece of **cucumber**, cut into strips

1 green eating **apple**, cut into thin wedges

Dressing – choose from page 36

---

1. Make the salad dressing. Set to one side until needed.
2. Mix together the hummus ingredients and blitz with a hand-held blender. Season with salt and pepper.
3. Beat the eggs in a bowl and add the flour, cumin and coriander. Beat together. Season well with salt and pepper.
4. Squeeze the excess water from the grated onions and carrots, add to the egg mixture and mix well.
5. Heat a little oil in a frying pan and add the pancake mix, 1 tablespoon at a time. Fry on each side for 1–2 minutes on a medium heat. Repeat until the pancake mix is used up.
6. Serve the hummus with the pancakes and salad.

Chilli Egg Fried Rice

£1.23 /PERSON

1/3 mug **basmati rice**

2 **carrots**, cut into small cubes

2 tablespoons **toasted sesame oil**

2 **eggs**, beaten

5 **spring onions**

1 clove **garlic**, chopped

1 **fat red chilli**, chopped

1 **pak choi**, sliced

1 mug defrosted **frozen peas**

1/2 tin **haricot beans**

1 tablespoon **soy sauce**

PREP 20 MINS

1. Put the rice and carrots in a saucepan with 2/3 mug of boiling water. Simmer for 10 minutes with the lid on the pan. The liquid should be absorbed into the rice.

2. Heat one tablespoon of toasted sesame oil in a frying pan or wok. Add the eggs and allow it to spread around the pan. It should form a thin omelette. Leave until the egg is set. Remove from the pan, roll up and cut into slices. Set aside until needed.

3. Add the other tablespoon of oil to the pan and fry the spring onions, garlic and chilli for 30 seconds. Add the pak choi and fry for 1 minute, stirring frequently.

4. Add the rice, carrots, peas, beans and soy and fry for 30 seconds.

5. Serve with the sliced, egg rolls on top.

Rice Noodles

Sauce

2 tablespoons **smooth peanut butter**

2 tablespoons **oil**

2 tablespoons **soy sauce**

1 tablespoon **white wine vinegar**

1 tablespoon freshly grated **ginger**

¼ mug **water**

½ x 200g packet **ribbon rice noodles**

1 tablespoon **oil**

1 medium **carrot**, cut into matchsticks

100g **mangetout**, sliced lengthways

100g **mushrooms**, sliced

1 **red pepper**, sliced thinly

140g **Quorn pieces**

£1.73 /PERSON

1

2

PREP 20 MINS

1. Mix together the sauce ingredients in a small bowl.
2. Put the rice noodles in a large bowl and pour over enough boiling water to cover them. Leave to stand for 7–8 minutes. Drain.
3. Heat the oil in a wok or large frying pan. Add the carrots and peppers and fry on a fairly high heat for 1 minute.
4. Add the mangetout, mushrooms and Quorn and fry for 1 minute.
5. Add the sauce and heat through, approx. 30 seconds.
6. Stir through the drained noodles.

something for the weekend

Got a little more time on your hands and fancy something a bit different to eat? Treat yourself to something from this section.

something for the weekend

Korma Beans with Naan

A spicy twist on the traditional beans on toast. If you like your food really spicy, try different curry pastes.

1 tablespoon **oil** to fry

1 medium **onion**, cut into thin wedges

1/2 **green pepper**, cut into thin slices

1 tablespoon **Korma curry paste**

4 medium **tomatoes**, cut into chunks

400g **cannellini beans**, rinsed and drained

1 tablespoon chopped, **fresh coriander**

2 **peshwari naan breads**

yogurt to serve

£1.34 /PERSON

2

2

PREP 15 MINS

1. Preheat the oven to 200°C fan oven/220°C/Gas 7. Put the naan bread in the oven for 3 minutes (check packet instructions).

2. Heat the oil in a frying pan, add the onions and peppers, and fry for 2–3 minutes, or until they are golden brown.

3. Add the curry paste and cook on a medium heat for 30 seconds, stirring frequently.

4. Add the tomatoes and beans and cook for a further 1 minute, stirring frequently. Add the coriander.

5. Serve with the warmed naan breads and a tablespoon of yogurt.

Spaghetti Bolognese

If you want to vary this recipe, you can add half a teaspoon of Marmite or HP sauce at stage 2.

£0.65 /PERSON

2

2

PREP 30 MINS

1 small **onion**, chopped

1 small **carrot**, finely chopped

1 **celery stick**, chopped

½ **red pepper**, chopped

1 tablespoon **oil** to fry

2 tablespoons **red lentils**

400g can **chopped tomatoes**

1 teaspoon **oregano**

1 mug **water** + 1 **vegetable stock cube**, crumbled

2 portions of **spaghetti** to serve (see page 23)

grated **Parmesan-style** or **Cheddar cheese** to serve

1. Heat the oil in a saucepan and fry the onion, carrot, celery and pepper for 3–4 minutes.

2. Add the lentils, tomatoes, oregano, stock cube and water. Bring to the boil. Season with salt and pepper. Leave to simmer for about 20 minutes until all the vegetables are cooked.

3. In the meantime, put the spaghetti on to cook (see page 23).

4. Drain the spaghetti and serve the Bolognese mixture on the top.

5. Grate some Parmesan-style or Cheddar cheese over the top.

Chilli Courgette Torte

Eat it on its own, with green salad, or one of the other salads in this book.

1 tablespoon **oil** to fry

2 medium **courgettes**, sliced

1 small **onion**, chopped

1 fresh **green chilli**, chopped

2 **eggs**

½ teaspoon **paprika**

½ mug grated **Cheddar cheese**

£0.82 /PERSON

2

2

PREP 15 MINS

COOK 25 MINS

1. Preheat the oven to 170°C fan oven/190°C/Gas 5. Grease a casserole dish.

2. Heat the oil in a frying pan and fry the courgettes. Transfer to a casserole dish.

3. Fry the onion and the chilli until they begin to brown. Add to the casserole dish.

4. Beat the eggs, then add the paprika to them. Pour the egg mixture over the courgettes. Sprinkle the cheese over the top. Bake in the oven for 25–30 minutes until the cheese has browned and the eggs are set.

Parsnip and Swede Bake

£1.60 /PERSON

3

2

PREP 20 MIN

COOK 30 MINS

2 tablespoons **olive oil**

1 **red onion**, sliced

1 small **swede**, cut into 2cm chunks

150g **chestnut mushrooms**, chopped

½ mug/150ml **water**

½ **vegetable stock cube**

1 clove **garlic**, chopped

½ teaspoon **dried thyme**

1 tablespoon **tomato purée**

50g packet **macadamia nuts**

½ tablespoon **wholegrain mustard**

125ml **crème fraîche**

1 medium **parsnip**, grated

1 medium **potato**, grated

1. Preheat the oven to 180ºC fan oven/200ºC/gas 6. Grease 2 individual, ovenproof dishes or 1 medium one.

2. Heat the oil in a large frying pan and fry the onions until they begin to soften. Season well with salt and pepper. Add the swede to the pan and cook over a medium heat for five minutes, stirring frequently.

3. Add the mushrooms and fry for 2–3 minutes.

4. Add the water, stock, garlic, thyme, tomato purée, macadamias and mustard and simmer gently for 10 minutes.

5. Stir in the crème fraîche and divide between the dishes. Top with the potato and parsnip.

6. Bake in the oven for 25–30 minutes, the tops should be lightly browned.

Sweet and Spicy Pilau

This is an appetizing rice salad, full of good things. Good to eat on its own as a snack, or with some green salad.

1 tablespoon **oil** to fry

1 **onion**, sliced

½ mug **basmati rice**

1½ mugs **water**

½ teaspoon **chilli powder**

¼ mug **currants**

¼ mug **ready-to-eat apricots**, chopped

¼ mug **sultanas**, currants, or raisins

¼ mug **pine nuts** or **almonds**

£1.12 /PERSON

2

2

PREP 30 MINS

1. Heat the oil in a saucepan and fry the onions until they become caramelised (go quite brown).

2. Add the rice, water and chilli powder. Bring to the boil, then turn down to simmer for about 10–15 minutes, uncovered, until the rice is cooked and the water has been absorbed.

3. Take off the heat and stir in the fruit and nuts.

Spinach, Bean and Potato Bake

Take care not to overcook the spinach, as it just needs to wilt a little.

£1.80 /PERSON

3

3-4

PREP 20 MINS

COOK 20 MINS

1 medium **potato**, cut into bite-sized pieces

½ **butternut squash**, cut into bite-sized pieces

2cm cube **butter**

1 tablespoon **oil** to fry

200g pack fresh **spinach**

1 **onion**, sliced

100g pack **pine nuts**

2 teaspoons **cumin seeds**

2 teaspoons **honey**

400g tin **cannellini beans**, washed and drained

1. Preheat the oven to 180°C fan oven/200°C/Gas 6.

2. Put the potatoes and squash on to simmer for 8 minutes. Drain, return to the pan and add the butter. Shake around to distribute evenly.

3. Heat a little oil in a wok and add the spinach. Fry for ½–1 minute until the spinach is wilted, but not mushy. Tip into the bottom of a casserole dish.

4. Heat a little oil in the wok and add the onions and pine nuts. Fry until they brown a little.

5. Add the fennel seeds, honey and drained beans. Mix together and then place on top of the spinach in the casserole dish.

6. Put the potato mix on top. Place in the oven for 20 minutes until the top is slightly browned.

Polenta and Roast Mushrooms

20g **butter**, cut into small cubes (measure using packet)

1 tablespoon **oil**

200g **chestnut mushrooms**, thickly sliced

2 **cloves garlic**, sliced

1 **red onion**, sliced

¼ mug **fine polenta**

1 mug boiling **water**

1 **veg stock cube**

¼ mug grated **Cheddar cheese**

£1.21 /PERSON

3

4

PREP 25 MINS

COOK 55 MINS

1. Preheat the oven to 180ºC fan oven/200ºC/gas 6.

2. Put the butter and oil in a roasting tray. Add the mushrooms, garlic and onions and mix together. Season with salt and pepper. Roast in the oven for 40 minutes.

3. About 10 minutes before the end of the cooking time, put the polenta, boiling water and stock cube in a saucepan and whisk together. Gently bring to the boil, stirring frequently. Simmer gently for 10 minutes, stirring frequently.

4. After 10 minutes, add the cheese and stir until the cheese melts.

5. Serve with the roasted mushrooms.

Potato and Nut Terrine

Serve with baked potatoes, salads, or one of the sauces on pages 32 and 33. You can eat it hot or cold, so it's OK to have for lunches and snacks the next day.

£1.75 /PERSON

3

4

PREP 25 MINS

COOK 55 MINS

2 medium **potatoes**, diced

1 **red onion**, chopped

2 **cloves garlic**, chopped

4–5 **mushrooms**, chopped

1 tablespoon **oil** to fry

1 tablespoon **curry paste**

4 **eggs**, beaten

1/2 x 250g pack of **cream cheese**, softened

200g pack of **pecan nuts**, roughly chopped

200g pack of **cashew nuts**, roughly chopped

1/2 mug grated **Parmesan-style cheese**

serve with **salad**

1. Preheat the oven to 170°C fan oven/190°C/Gas 5. Grease a loaf tin and put a piece of greaseproof paper across the bottom.

2. Cook the potatoes in boiling water for 10 minutes. Drain and mash slightly with a fork. It does not need to be smooth.

3. Fry the onions, garlic and mushrooms in the oil for 4–5 minutes until they are softened. Add the curry paste and stir well. Add this to the potatoes in the saucepan, along with the eggs, cream cheese, nuts and Parmesan. Season well and mix together.

4. Put the mixture into the loaf tin and bake in the oven for 45 minutes. Serve, hot or cold, with a sauce or salad.

If you like your loaf nutty, check out this fennel and chestnut loaf! noshbooks.com/nutty-loaf

Nut and Courgette Slice

The slice is served here with salad and a yogurt dressing (page 37).

1 tablespoon **oil** to fry

1 small **onion**, chopped

1 **clove garlic**, chopped

2 **eggs**, beaten

2 tablespoons **milk**

1 slice **bread** made into breadcrumbs

1 large **courgette**, grated

1 small **carrot**, grated

200g pack mixed **chopped nuts**

½ mug grated **Cheddar cheese**

£1.38 /PERSON

2

2

PREP 15 MINS

COOK 40 MINS

1. Preheat the oven to 180°C fan oven/200°C/Gas 6. Grease a loaf tin and put a piece of greaseproof paper on the bottom.

2. Heat a little oil in a frying pan and fry the onion and garlic in a saucepan for 2–3 minutes.

3. Take off the heat. Add the rest of the ingredients, season and mix well.

4. Pour into the loaf tin and press down evenly. Bake in the oven for 35–40 minutes until browned on top.

5. Leave to cool in the tin. Serve sliced with salad and a dressing (see page 36).

Mediterranean Bulgar Wheat Salad

Use up any leftover feta in sandwiches. Great with tomatoes.

£1.07 /PERSON

1

2-3

PREP 30 MINS

½ mug **bulgar wheat**

1 **vegetable stock cube** + ¾ mug boiling **water**

6 **cherry tomatoes**, each cut in ½

3 **spring onions**, chopped

1 medium **avocado**, peeled and cut into wedges

12 **olives**, halved

½ x 200g pack **feta**, cut into small cubes

½ **red pepper**, sliced thinly

green salad

Dressing

1 tablespoon **olive oil**

juice of ½ **lemon**

1 teaspoon **sugar**

1 dessertspoon chopped **fresh basil**

salt and **pepper**

---

1. Put the bulgar wheat in a pan with the boiling water and stock cube. Simmer for 5 minutes until the liquid is absorbed. Allow to cool.

2. Mix the dressing ingredients together and set aside until needed.

3. Arrange the green salad on individual plates.

4. Mix the tomatoes, olives, spring onions and pepper into the cooled bulgar wheat. Arrange over the salad.

5. Put the avocado and feta cheese over the bulgar wheat and drizzle the dressing over.

Onion and Squash Pie

4 **medium potatoes**, cut into 2cm cubes

2 tablespoons **oil**

2 **onions**, sliced

1/2 **butternut squash**, cut into small chunks

1/2 **fat red chilli**, chopped

1 mug grated **gruyère cheese** (can use **Cheddar**)

1/2 mug **cashews**, roughly chopped

375g **ready-rolled puff pastry**

egg, beaten

£2.19 /PERSON

5

2-3

PREP 25 MINS

COOK 30 MINS

1. Preheat the oven to 200ºC fan oven/220ºC/gas 7.

2. Put the potatoes on a roasting tray, season with salt and pepper, drizzle over a tablespoon of oil. Mix everything together and spread out the potatoes. Roast in the oven for 45 minutes.

3. Heat a tablespoon of oil in a large frying pan, add the onions and fry for 3-4 minutes on a medium heat. Add the squash and continue to fry for another 3-4 minutes. Things should begin to brown. Season with salt and pepper. Add the chilli, cheese and cashews and mix. Take off the heat.

4. Unroll the puff pastry onto a large, greased baking tray.

5. Wet the edges of the pastry to help them stick together. Pour the frying pan contents onto one side of the pastry, then fold the other side over the top. Pinch together the edges and brush the top with the beaten egg.

6. Bake in the oven for 25-30 minutes. The top should be golden brown.

7. Serve with the potatoes.

Goat's Cheese Tart with Green Olives

You can use the base of this tart almost like a pizza. Add a tomato sauce (see pages 32 & 33), plus some vegetables and cheese and invent your own pizzas.

£1.32 /PERSON

3

2

PREP 15 MINS

COOK 25 MINS

Base

1 tablespoon **oil** to fry

½ **onion**, finely chopped

1 mug **self-raising flour**

50g **butter**, measure using packet

1 **egg**, beaten

Topping

8 **cherry tomatoes**

15–18 **green olives,** halved

125g packet of **soft goat's cheese**

salad to serve

French dressing (see page 36)

1. Heat a little oil in a frying pan and fry the onion until it begins to brown. Set aside.

2. Preheat the oven to 180°C fan oven/200°C/Gas 6.

3. Put the flour in a bowl and rub in the butter. Add the onions and the beaten egg. If the mixture is still dry, add a little milk.

4. Tip out onto a surface and squash together. Place on a greased baking tray and squash out gently with your fingers to make a round. It should be about 1cm thick.

5. Cut the tomatoes in half and spread over the top with the olives and the crumbled cheese. Drizzle oil over the top.

6. Bake in the oven for 25 minutes. Serve with salad and sprinkle some French dressing (see page 36) over the tart.

Savoury Pancakes

Savoury pancakes are made in exactly the same way as sweet ones. Add savoury fillings and they can turn from fun food to a serious meal.

£1.03 /PERSON

2

2

PREP 25 MINS

2 **eggs**

6 tablespoons **self-raising flour** (you can use one half bulgar wheat flour and one half self-raising flour)

milk

Trex or white Flora to fry (you can use oil but a lard type is best)

Filling

1 tablespoon **oil** to fry

1 **red onion**, sliced

1/2 **green pepper**, chopped

1/2 **red pepper**, chopped

4 **mushrooms**, sliced

Quick Cheese Sauce (page 33)

1. Make the pancakes in the same way as on page 198.
2. Heat the oil in a frying pan. Add the onions and fry until they begin to brown. Add the peppers and mushroom and fry for a further 2–3 minutes.
3. Serve with the Quick Cheese Sauce.

Tofu Balls with Tomato Sauce

A good recipe to make tofu a bit more tasty. The tomato sauce is essential.

Tofu balls

1 small **onion**, finely chopped

1 small **garlic clove**, finely chopped

½ x 375g pack **tofu**, chopped

1 **slice of bread** made into breadcrumbs

1 **egg yoke**

1 tablespoon **flour**

1 tablespoon **soy sauce**

1 teaspoon **dried chives**

1 teaspoon **dried basil**

Tomato sauce

1 tablespoon **oil** to fry

1 **clove garlic**, finely chopped

1 medium **onion**, chopped

400g can **chopped tomatoes**

1 tablespoon **tomato purée**

rice to serve (see page 22)

£1.03 /PERSON

2

2

PREP 15 MINS

COOK 30 MINS

1. Preheat the oven to 180°C fan oven/200°C/Gas 6.

2. Put all the tofu balls ingredients together in a bowl and mix well. Form into balls and place on a greased baking tray. Cook in the oven for 25–30 minutes until they are browned.

3. While they are cooking, put the rice on to cook (see page 22).

4. To make the sauce, fry the onions and garlic in a saucepan and add the tomatoes and tomato purée. Cook for about 5 minutes. Season with salt and pepper. Whizz with the blender.

Roast Vegetable with Chunky Tofu

Tofu is high in protein and contains calcium, iron and Vitamins B1, B2 and B3. It is, however, fairly bland in taste and therefore needs to be eaten with other, more tasty, foods.

½ x 350g block of **tofu**

½ **onion** cut into wedges

1 small **sweet potato**, peeled and cut into small chunks

4 **mushrooms**, sliced

2 **tomatoes**, cut into 4

½ **red pepper**, chopped

½ **fat red chilli**, chopped

1 teaspoon **rosemary** (optional)

1 tablespoon **oil**

£1.45 /PERSON

1

1

PREP 10 MINS

COOK 45 MINS

1. Preheat the oven to 180°C fan oven/200°C/Gas 6.

2. Cut the tofu up into chunks.

3. Place all the ingredients into a casserole dish, sprinkle over with olive oil and mix to cover all the ingredients in oil.

4. Season with salt and pepper and sprinkle with rosemary if you have some. Bake in the oven for 45 minutes until nicely browned.

Red Chilli Tofu

This won't reheat well, so best shared with a friend.

1 tablespoon **oil** to fry

1 **onion**, chopped

1 **clove garlic**, chopped

349g pack firm **tofu**, cubed

1 **fat red chilli**, chopped

2 tablespoons **soy sauce**

1 tablespoon **white wine vinegar**

1 teaspoon **sugar** or **honey**

300g tin **broad beans**, drained. Try to get frozen soy beans.

1 teaspoon **dried coriander**

rice to serve (see page 22)

£1.56 /PERSON

2

2

PREP 25 MINS

1. Put the rice on to cook (see page 22).
2. Heat the oil in a wok and add the onions, garlic and tofu, Fry until browned.
3. Add the chilli and fry for 30 seconds.
4. Add the rest of the ingredients and cook for 2 minutes, on a high heat, stirring frequently.
5. Serve with rice.

friends around

Want to impress your friends, but not sure how? Here is something for when there is a hungry crowd to feed.

friends around

Fried Halloumi Salad with Pine Nut Couscous

Bags of green salad are very convenient. A cheaper way is to buy a small lettuce, some cucumber and spring onions. This will make a larger quantity for about the same price.

£2.22 /PERSON

1

2-3

PREP 25 MINS

½ mug **couscous**

½ **vegetable stock cube** + 1 mug boiling **water**

4 **spring onions**, chopped

1 **red apple**, chopped

½ x 100g pack of **pine nuts**

2 sticks **celery**, chopped

1 tablespoon **oil** to fry

250g pack of **halloumi cheese**, sliced

Dressing

2 tablespoons **olive oil**

juice of a **lemon**

2 tablespoons chopped fresh **mint**

1 teaspoon **sugar**

salt and **pepper**

green salad

1. Put the couscous in a bowl and add the water and stock cube. Stir and cover. Leave for 4–5 minutes.

2. Once cooled, add the onions, apple, celery and pine nuts.

3. Mix the dressing ingredients together and set to one side.

4. Heat the oil in a frying pan and fry the halloumi, on a fairly high heat, until it becomes browned.

5. Arrange the green salad on the individual plates. Put the couscous mix over the top and place the halloumi on top of the couscous. Drizzle over with the dressing.

Mango and Noodle Salad

This is best served hot, since it does not reheat well. You can use the leftover mango from this recipe in a smoothie.

£1.10 /PERSON

2

2

PREP 15 MINS

½ ripe **mango**

1 tablespoon **oil** to fry

3 **spring onions**, chopped

1 clove **garlic**, chopped

½ **red pepper**, sliced

½ **yellow pepper**, sliced

½ **red chilli**, deseeded and chopped

½ x 200g pack of ready-to-eat **rice noodles**

Dressing

2 tablespoons peanut butter

⅓ mug coconut milk

½ teaspoon tomato purée

1. Peel the mango and cut into strips.

2. To make the dressing, just mix the ingredients together until smooth.

3. Heat the oil in a frying pan. Fry the onions, garlic, peppers and chilli for 4–5 minutes. The onions should be softened.

4. Add the mango and the noodles. Cook for 1 minute, stirring frequently. Once everything is heated through, transfer to serving plates and pour the peanut sauce over the top.

Nut and Carrot Coleslaw

You can eat this with other salads, or with baked potatoes and cheese. It is so much better than coleslaw you might buy, ready-made, from a supermarket. If you want to keep half for the next day, divide in 2 before you put the dressing on.

£0.60 /PERSON

1

2

PREP 15 MINS

Dressing

3 tablespoons **olive oil**

1 tablespoon **chives**

2 tablespoons **white wine vinegar**

1 teaspoon **sugar**

salt and **pepper**

1 **carrot**, grated

3 **spring onions**, cut into long strips

2 **celery** sticks, chopped

¼ **Chinese cabbage**, thinly sliced

½ mug **cashew nuts**

1. Mix together the dressing ingredients.
2. Put all the other ingredients in a bowl and mix with a spoon. Pour the dressing over and mix.

Fruit'n Nut Salad

This salad has lots of healthy things in it. It has a yummy, crunchy, sweet-and-savoury flavour. You can eat it as a snack by itself, or to accompany vegetarian sausages or bean burgers.

£1.62 /PERSON

2

2-3

PREP 25 MINS

¾ mug basmati **rice**, cooked in 1½ mugs water with 1 teaspoon **pilau rice seasoning**

1 tablespoon **oil** to fry

1 medium **onion**, chopped

1 tablespoon **turmeric**

1 teaspoon **curry paste**

grated rind of 1 **lemon**

½ mug **pine nuts**

½ mug **dates**, chopped

½ mug ready-to-eat **figs**, chopped

2 sticks **celery**, chopped

4 heaped tablespoons **mayonnaise**

juice of a **lemon**

½ mug **pecan nuts**, roughly chopped

1. Cook the rice with the pilau rice seasoning (see page 22).

2. Fry the onions until they begin to brown. Add the turmeric and curry paste and mix well. Cook for 2–3 minutes. Add the rest of the ingredients and mix.

Spanish Baked Eggs

Best cooked for 2 and shared, since the eggs won't reheat too well. You can eat it cold with some salad. You could also eat it with some vegetarian sausages.

2 large **potatoes**, washed and diced

1 tablespoon **oil** to fry

1 small **onion**, cut into wedges

1 clove **garlic**, chopped

1/2 **green pepper**, chopped

400g can **chopped tomatoes**

1/2 teaspoon **paprika**

1 teaspoon **dried chives**

18 pitted **black olives**

4 **eggs**

£ /PER
2
2
PREP 15 MINS
COOK 15 MINS

1. Preheat the oven to 200°C fan oven/220°C/Gas 7.

2. Add the potatoes to a pan of boiling water and simmer for 10 minutes. Drain.

3. Heat the oil in a frying pan and cook the onion, garlic and peppers for 2–3 minutes. Add the tomatoes, paprika, chives and olives. Cook for 2 minutes. Add the potatoes and mix well.

4. Place in a greased casserole dish. Make 4 hollows in the mixture and break an egg into each. Season with salt and pepper.

5. Bake in the oven for 15 minutes, or until the eggs are cooked.

a

...od for feeding large numbers of people. Just multiply these ...cordingly. You can obviously vary the vegetables you use. Any ...s will need to be precooked.

£1.44 /PERSON

5

3-4

PREP 25 MINS

COOK 35 MINS

1 tablespoon **oil** to fry

1 small **onion**, chopped

1 clove **garlic**, chopped

1/2 **red pepper**, sliced

4 **mushrooms**, sliced

2 sticks **celery**, sliced

1 small **aubergine**, cut into chunks

1 small **courgette**, sliced

400g tin **chopped tomatoes**

1 teaspoon **mixed herbs**

2 x quantity of **Quick Cheese Sauce** (see page 33)

6 **lasagna sheets**

1/2 mug grated **Cheddar cheese**

1. Preheat the oven to 180°C fan oven/200°C/Gas 6.

2. Heat the oil in a wok and fry the onion, garlic, peppers, mushrooms, celery, aubergine and courgette for 4–5 minutes. Add the tin of tomatoes, and the herbs, and bring to the boil. Simmer for 5 minutes.

3. Make the double quantity of Quick Cheese Sauce (see page 33).

4. Put half the vegetable mixture in the bottom of a casserole dish. Cover with one layer of lasagna strips. Pour half the cheese sauce over. Cover with another layer of lasagna strips. Put the rest of the vegetables on top. Cover with another layer of lasagna strips. Pour over the rest of the cheese sauce. Top with the grated cheese.

5. Cook in the oven for 25–30 minutes. Test the pasta to see if it is cooked. If it has not, turn the oven down to 160°C fan oven/180°C/Gas 4 and cook for another 5–10 minutes.

6. Serve with salad.

Chickpea Patties with Yogurt Dressing

£0.85 /PERSON

3

2

PREP 25 MINS

Chickpeas are an important source of protein. If you want to use any of the patties for the next day, leave them unfried and keep them covered in the fridge.

Patties	Yogurt sauce	Spicy onions
400g tin of **chickpeas**, rinsed and drained	3 tablespoons **natural yogurt**	1 tablespoon **oil** to fry
½ **onion**, grated	1 tablespoon **mango** or **fruit chutney**	1 large **onion**, sliced
1 small **courgette**, grated	1 teaspoon **mint**	1 **fat red chilli**, deseeded and sliced
1 slice of **wholemeal bread**, made into breadcrumbs		
1 **egg**, beaten		
1 teaspoon dried **chives**		
1 tablespoon **oil** to fry		

1. Roughly mash the drained chickpeas with a fork.

2. Squeeze the water out of the grated onion. Mix the onion together in a bowl with the grated courgette, chives and chickpeas.

3. Mix the egg and breadcrumbs together in a separate bowl or mug. This helps the bread to soak and mix more easily with the other ingredients. Season with salt and pepper, add to the chickpea and mix. The mixture should be fairly stiff. Tip out onto a surface and, with floured hands, form 4 patties.

4. Heat the oil in a frying pan and put the patties in to fry. Keep the heat moderate and cook for about 5 minutes each side.

5. While they are cooking, mix the yogurt sauce ingredients together.

6. To make the spicy onions, fry the sliced onions in a saucepan on a fairly high heat. Allow them to brown, then add the chilli and mix well. Cook for 1 minute and then take off the heat.

Koftas with Mango Yogurt Dip

These have 5 stars because they are fiddly and take some time to make, not because they are particularly difficult. My family devoured these as soon as the photograph was taken. The yogurt dressing really makes the dish, so don't miss out on it.

£0.65 /PERSON

5

3-4

PREP 30 MINS

COOK 20 MINS

1 tablespoon **oil** to fry

1/2 **onion**, finely chopped

1 clove **garlic**, finely chopped

1 **carrot**, finely chopped

1 **celery** stick, finely chopped

1 **chilli**, deseeded and chopped

1½ mugs **water**

1 **vegetable stock cube**

1 dessertspoon **curry paste**

2/3 mug **red lentils**

1 tablespoon **tomato purée**

1/3 mug **cashews**

1 mug fresh **breadcrumbs**

1 small **egg**, beaten

salt and **pepper**

Yogurt dip

3 tablespoons **natural yogurt**

1 tablespoon **mango chutney**

1 teaspoon **coriander** or **oregano**

1. Heat the oil in a saucepan. Fry the onions, garlic, carrot, celery and chilli for 2–3 minutes until the onions start to soften.

2. Add the water, crumbled stock cube, curry paste, lentils and tomato purée. Bring to the boil. Turn down to simmer, with the lid on, for 20 minutes. Check every now and then to see that it has not boiled dry and to stir. If, after the 20 minutes, it is still very wet, cook for a further 5 minutes with the lid off. The mixture should be like a paste. Leave to cool.

3. Chop or whizz the cashew nuts, but not too fine. Crumble the breadcrumbs (you could whizz with the blender). Add the bread, egg, coriander, nuts and seasoning to the mixture in the pan. Stir well.

4. Preheat the oven to 160°C fan oven/180°C/Gas 4.

5. Grease a baking tray. Spoon the dessertspoons of the mixture onto the greased baking tray and form them into balls, see photo. It should make about 20. Put in the oven for 15–20 minutes until they are brown.

6. Mix the dip ingredients together and serve with the hot koftas.

Cannelloni

This is dinner party food. It is so fiddly to fill the cannelloni shells, hence the 5 star rating, but is well worth the effort. Italian in origin, excellent food and bound to impress any guests.

1 tablespoon **oil** to fry

$^1/_2$ **onion**, chopped

1 clove **garlic**, chopped

handful of **spinach**, torn into large pieces

300g pack of **cream cheese** (soft cheese)

2 tablespoons grated **Parmesan-style cheese**

8 **cannelloni shells**

2 extra tablespoons grated **Parmesan-style cheese,** for sprinkling on top

1 quantity of **Tomato Sauce** (see page 33). You could use the Quick Cheese Sauce on page 33 instead of the Tomato Sauce.

1. Preheat the oven to 180°C fan oven/200°C/Gas 6.

2. Make the Tomato Sauce (see page 33).

3. Heat the oil in a frying pan and fry the onion and garlic until the onions are soft. Add the spinach and cook until it wilts, approximately 1 minute.

4. Mix the cream cheese and Parmesan together in a bowl and soften with a fork. Add the onion and spinach mixture. Mix. Use this mixture to fill the cannelloni shells. Spoon into the top of the cannelloni tubes and push in with the handle of a small spoon. Repeat the process until the shell is completely full. Your hands will get very messy.

5. Place in a greased casserole dish or shallow, ovenproof dish and cover with the Tomato Sauce, or the Quick Cheese Sauce. Cook in the oven for 15 minutes. Sprinkle the rest of the Parmesan over the top and cook for another 10 minutes. Serve immediately.

Two Cheese and Spinach Loaf

You could spread this with butter and eat with more cheese and pickles. You could also put half in the freezer, once it is cooled, as the loaf is quite big.

2cm cube **butter**

1 **leek**, chopped

50g **fresh spinach**

1½ mugs **self-raising flour**

salt and **pepper**

¾ mug **Parmesan-style cheese**

1 mug grated **Cheddar cheese**

1 teaspoon **basil**

1 **egg**, beaten + **milk** to make

¾ mug liquid

£2.68 /TOTAL

3

8

PREP 15 MINS

COOK 30 MINS

1. Preheat the oven to 180°C fan oven/200°C/Gas 6.

2. Heat the butter in a frying pan and fry the leeks. When they are soft, add the spinach and cook for about 30 seconds until it wilts.

3. In a bowl, mix the flour, salt and pepper, cheeses and basil. Add the leeks and spinach from the frying pan. Mix.

4. Add the egg and milk and mix until it forms a ball in the bowl. You do not necessarily need to use all the liquid. It should not be too sticky.

5. Grease a loaf tin and then press the mixture evenly into it. Bake in the oven for 35–40 minutes. Once cooked, leave to cool and then slice.

Pistachio Hummus

100g **pistachios**

25ml **olive oil**

juice of a **lemon**

100ml **Greek-style yoghurt**

1 **fat red chilli**, deseeded and chopped

200g **feta**, crumbled

carrot

cucumber

celery

£0.92 /PERSON

1

2-3

PREP 15 MINS

1. Blend the pistachios with a hand-held blender. Add the oil, lemon, yogurt and chilli and blend for another 30 seconds.

2. Crumble in the feta and mix by hand.

3. Serve with the vegetables cut into sticks.

Hoisin Wrap

1 tablespoon **oil**

½ **onion**, sliced

½ **red pepper**, sliced

½ **fat red chilli**, deseeded and chopped

2 **mushrooms**, sliced

6 pieces **baby corn**, sliced lengthways

3 tablespoons **hoisin** sauce

2 **tortillas**

£2.12 /PERSON

2

1

PREP 15 MINS

1. Heat the oil in a frying pan. Fry the onion and pepper for 2 minutes.

2. Add the chilli, baby corn and mushrooms and fry for one minute.

3. Add the hoisin sauce and cook gently for 1 minute.

4. Divide between the two tortillas.

142 friends around

Persian Pilaf

1 tablespoon **oil**

1 medium **red onion**, sliced

1 clove **garlic**, chopped

1 medium **carrot**, cut into dice

1 medium **leek**, sliced

½ mug **basmati rice**

1 ½ mugs **water** + 1 **veg stock cube**

½ mug **pistachios**

⅓ mug **raisins**

½ teaspoon **turmeric**

½ teaspoon **coriander**

½ tin **green lentils**

£1.25 /PERSON

2

2

PREP 20 MINS

1. Heat the oil in a frying pan and fry the onion, garlic, carrot and leek for 2 minutes.

2. Add the rice and fry for 30 seconds. Add the water, stock cube, pistachios, raisins and spices. Bring to the boil and turn down to simmer, with a lid on the pan, for 10 minutes. Season well with salt and pepper.

3. Add the lentils and simmer for a further 5 minutes with the lid on the pan.

Nachos

Nachos are so quick to make and are excellent for parties, or snacks while you are relaxing, watching a video, etc.

½ x 200g packet of **corn chips**, plain or flavoured

1½ mugs of grated **cheese**

dipping salsa sauce (see page 147)

£0.94 /PERSON

1

2-3

PREP 10 MINS

COOK 3 MINS

1. Heat the oven to 220°C fan oven/240°C/Gas 9.
2. Pile the chips on an ovenproof plate.
3. Sprinkle the grated cheese on the top and cover the chips.
4. Place in the oven for 2–3 minutes only. The cheese only needs to melt, it does not need to brown.
5. Pour the salsa over the top, serve and eat immediately.

Salsa

If you are having a party, these will work out much cheaper than the bought variety. Salsa is good with tortilla chips, quesidillas, and big wraps. If you like your salsa really hot, then adjust the amount of chilli powder or chilli flakes.

Dipping Salsa

£0.80 TOTAL

1 tablespoon **oil** to fry

1 **onion**, finely chopped

3 **cloves garlic**, finely chopped

400g tin of **chopped tomatoes**

½ tablespoon **tomato purée**

1 teaspoon **chilli flakes**

½ teaspoon **paprika**

1 teaspoon **sugar**

2 teaspoons **dried chives**

1. Heat a little oil in a saucepan and fry the onions and garlic in a pan, until they begin to brown.

2. Add the tin of tomatoes and bring to the boil. Add the tomato purée, chilli, paprika and sugar. Simmer gently for 3–4 minutes. Add the chives.

Avocado Salsa

£1.37 TOTAL

1 medium **avocado**, peeled and chopped into small pieces

1 medium **onion**, finely chopped

2 medium **tomatoes**, chopped into small pieces

½ teaspoon **chilli powder**

¼ teaspoon **paprika**

½ teaspoon **sugar**

1 teaspoon **lemon juice** (this stops the avocado from discolouring)

salt and **pepper**

Tomato and Onion Salsa

£1.10 TOTAL

4 **tomatoes**, cut into small pieces

1 **green chilli pepper**, chopped finely

½ **onion**, chopped finely

1 teaspoon **sugar**

1 teaspoon **lemon juice**

salt and **pepper**

For Avocado Salsa and Tomato and Onion Salsa, simply prepare the ingredients and mix together.

1

1+

PREP 10 MINS

Spinach and Cottage Cheese Lasagna

You could add an extra teaspoon of flour to the cheese sauce mix to make it less runny and the lasagna will hold together better.

£1.80 /PERSON

5

3-4

PREP 30 MINS

COOK 25 MINS

2 x **Quick Cheese Sauce** (page 33)

450g **cottage cheese**

1/2 mug grated **Cheddar cheese**

oil to fry

1 small **onion**, chopped

1 **clove garlic**, finely chopped

500g **fresh spinach**

juice of a 1/2 **lemon**

250g pack of **lasagna sheets**

1/2 mug grated **Cheddar cheese** for the top

crusty bread to serve

1. Preheat the oven to 180°C fan oven/200°C/Gas 6. Grease a casserole dish.

2. Make the Quick Cheese Sauce (see page 33).

3. Mix together 1/2 mug grated cheese and the cottage cheese.

4. Heat a little oil in a frying pan and add the onions and garlic. Fry until the onions begin to soften. Add the spinach and fry until it begins to wilt. Take off the heat and add the lemon juice. Season well with salt and pepper.

5. Put some of the cheese sauce in the bottom of the casserole dish, then a single layer of lasagna sheets, then add the cottage cheese mix, then another layer of lasagna sheets, then a layer of cheese sauce and finally another layer of lasagna sheets. Place the spinach mix on top, followed by another layer of lasagna sheets. Top with cheese sauce and lastly, the other 1/2 mug of grated cheese.

6. Place in the oven for 25 minutes. The cheese should be browned on the top and the lasagna sheets cooked.

7. Serve with crusty bread.

For another angle on the classic lasagna, why not try Joy's Mushroom Lasagna. The recipe is over at noshbooks.com/mushroom

Big Wraps

salsa (see page 145)

½ mug **rice** (see page 22)

1 tablespoon **oil** to fry

1 **onion**, finely chopped

4 **mushrooms**, cut into fairly small pieces

1 red, green or yellow **pepper**, chopped

½ x 350g **chicken-style Quorn**

1 small tin of **sweetcorn**

4 **tortilla wraps**

½ mug of finely grated strong **Cheddar cheese**

1 dessertspoon **soured cream**

£1.06 /PERSON

2

4

PREP 25 MINS

1. Make the salsa and cook the rice. Set to one side

2. Heat a little oil in a wok and fry the onions for 2–3 minutes until they begin to soften. Add the mushrooms and pepper and continue to cook for about 3 minutes.

3. Add the Quorn and cook for 1 minute.

4. Add the rice and the drained sweetcorn and cook for 2–3 minutes until everything is heated through. Season with salt and pepper. Take off the heat and leave in the pan to keep warm.

5. Gently warm the tortilla wraps under the grill on a low heat for 2 minutes, or in the microwave for 10 seconds.

6. Put ¼ of the filling onto each wrap and sprinkle the grated cheese on the top. Place a blob of the soured cream on top. Fold the tortilla over. Serve with the salsa.

Roast Wedges

This dish of oven-baked vegetables makes a good accompaniment to bean burgers, or vegetarian sausages, but can make a meal in itself.

1 large **potato**, cut into wedges

½ **yellow** or **red pepper**, sliced

2 **mushrooms**, sliced

2 **tomatoes**, cut into wedges

1 tablespoon **tomato purée**

1 teaspoon **chives**

¼ mug **water**
+ 1 **vegetable stock cube**

½ mug grated **cheese**

£0.69 /PERSON

2

2

PREP 10 MINS

COOK 20 MINS

1. Preheat the oven to 180°C fan oven/200°C/Gas 6.

2. Put the potato into a pan of boiling water and simmer for 10 minutes. Drain and put into a greased casserole dish.

3. Add the peppers, mushrooms and tomatoes.

4. Mix the tomato purée, chives, water and crumbled stock cube together in a mug or small bowl. Pour over the vegetables and mix. Season well.

5. Top with grated cheese and place in the oven for 15–20 minutes until the cheese is browned.

Curried Wedges

This is how to make chips the safe way, without deep frying. Also, they are slightly more healthy. If you don't want your chips spicy, just wedges, don't add the curry paste to the oil.

1 large **sweet potato**

2 large **potatoes**

¼ mug **oil**

1 teaspoon **curry paste**

1. Preheat the oven to 180°C fan oven/200°C/Gas 6.

2. You do not need to peel the potatoes, just wash them. Cut them all into wedges.

3. Place the chips on a baking tray. Using a mug, mix the curry paste with the oil and sprinkle over the chips. Toss the chips in the oil to make sure they are all covered. Spread them out on the tray.

4. Cook in the oven for 40 minutes. They should be nicely browned by this point.

5. Serve with your choice of dip.

£0.38 /PERSON

2

2

PREP 10 MINS

COOK 40 MINS

Chestnut Hot Pot

£2.07 /EACH

2

2

PREP 20 MINS

COOK 25 MINS

2 medium **potatoes**, cut into 2 cm chunks

³/₄ mug defrosted **frozen peas**

25g **butter** (measure using packet)

1 tablespoon **oil**

1 **onion**, sliced

2 sticks **celery**, sliced

1 clove **garlic**, chopped

4 **tomatoes**, chopped

1 **veg stock cube** + ¹/₂ mug **water**

180g pack **cooked whole chestnuts**, roughly chopped

1 tablespoon **tomato purée**

¹/₂ teaspoon **cumin**

¹/₂ teaspoon **coriander**

¹/₂ teaspoon **paprika**

1 **egg** beaten

1. Preheat the oven to 180ºC fan oven/200ºC/gas 6.
2. Put the potatoes in a pan of boiling water and simmer for 9 minutes. Add the peas and simmer for 1 minute. Drain and return to the pan with the butter and mash.
3. Heat the oil in a frying pan and add the onions, celery and garlic. Fry on a medium heat for 2–3 minutes.
4. Add the tomatoes and fry for 2 minutes.
5. Add the veg stock, water, chestnuts, tomato purée, cumin, coriander and paprika. Stir together and bring to the boil. Transfer into a small casserole dish.
6. Arrange the potato mixture over the top. Brush with the beaten egg.
7. Bake in the oven for 25 minutes, the top should be nicely browned.

Nutty Sweet Potato and Spinach Pie

Spinach only takes seconds to cook. As soon as it has wilted, take it out of the pan.

375g pack of **frozen, ready-rolled puff pastry**

2 large **sweet potatoes**, peeled and cut into chunks

2 x 2cm cube **butter**

1 tablespoon **oil** to fry

200g pack **fresh spinach**

1 tablespoon **oil** to fry

2 **onions**, sliced

100g pack **pine nuts**

2 teaspoons **fennel seeds**

1 teaspoon **honey**

1 **egg**, beaten

1. Preheat the oven to 200°C fan oven/220°C/Gas 7. Grease a 20cm x 13cm casserole dish.

2. Put the sweet potatoes in a pan of boiling water and simmer for 8 minutes. Drain and mash with a 2cm cube of butter and season with salt and pepper.

3. Heat a little oil in a wok and add the spinach. Cook for 30 seconds to wilt. Place the spinach on the bottom of the casserole dish.

4. Heat the other cube of butter and the oil in the wok. Add the sliced onions and pine nuts and fry until they begin to turn brown. Stir frequently. Add the fennel seeds and honey and fry for 30 seconds. Season with salt and pepper.

5. Place the mashed sweet potato on top of the spinach in the casserole dish. Spread evenly.

6. Place the onion mix on top of the sweet potato.

7. Unroll the pastry and cut a piece big enough to cover the top of the casserole dish. Place on the dish and pinch the edges. Brush with the beaten egg and place in the oven for 20 minutes until the pastry is golden brown.

comfort food

Want something to give you that warm, 'cosy' feeling, without spending too much money? Have yourself something wholesome.

Leek and Potato Soup

The recipe asks for double cream, but you can replace this with milk. It freezes well for another day.

2cm cube **butter** to fry

2 **leeks**, sliced

1 small **potato**, diced

1 small **carrot**, chopped

3 mugs **water** with 2 **vegetable stock cubes** crumbled in

2 tablespoons **double cream**

£0.78 /PERSON

2

2

PREP 10 MINS

COOK 20 MINS

1. Melt the butter in a saucepan and fry the vegetables for 4–5 minutes. Stir frequently.

2. Add the stock and water and bring to the boil. Turn down the heat and simmer for 15 minutes.

3. Using the hand-held blender, whizz until the soup is smooth.

4. Stir in the double cream and season with salt and pepper. Serve with crusty bread.

Classic Nut Roast

You can use a variety of nuts in this recipe, but cashews, macadamia or Brazil nuts seem to work the best. Any leftovers are ideal to eat cold the next day, but probably best not microwaved.

1 tablespoon **oil** to fry

1 small **onion**, chopped finely

2 **mushrooms**, chopped finely

200g pack **cashew nuts**, chopped

2 slices **wholemeal bread**

½ mug boiling **water**

¼ mug **vegetable stock**

1 teaspoon **Marmite**

1 teaspoon **mixed herbs**

£1.45
/PERSON

2

2

PREP
10 MINS

COOK
20 MINS

1. Preheat the oven to 180°C fan oven/200°C/Gas 6. Grease a small ovenproof dish.

2. Fry the onions in a little oil in a saucepan until they begin to brown. Add the mushrooms and cook for a further 2–3 minutes. Take off the heat. Add the chopped nuts to the pan.

3. Make the bread into breadcrumbs. Just rub it between your fingers; it does not matter if the breadcrumbs are a bit chunky. Add to the pan.

4. Add ½ a vegetable stock cube into ½ a mug of boiling water to make up the stock. Add the teaspoon of Marmite and stir until dissolved.

5. Add the herbs and the contents of the mug to the pan. Mix everything together.

6. Pour into the dish and cook for 20 minutes in the oven. The nuts should be brown on top.

7. Serve with salad, baked potatoes, pasta, or roasted vegetables. If you wish, serve with one of the sauces on pages 32 & 33.

Curried Split Pea Casserole

You need to decide on this one ahead of time, since the peas need to be soaked overnight and the cooking time is lengthy. The actual labour time is not. You can reheat any leftovers the next day.

1 tablespoon **oil** to fry

1 small **onion**, chopped

1 teaspoon grated **ginger**

1 clove of **garlic**, chopped

1 small **carrot**, grated

1/3 mug **yellow split peas**, soaked overnight

1 teaspoon **wholegrain mustard**

1 small **red chilli**, deseeded and chopped

1 dessertspoon **curry paste**

1 dessertspoon **tomato purée**

400g tin of **chopped tomatoes**

1 mug of **water** + 1 **vegetable stock cube**

2 **sweet potatoes**, peeled and cut into chunks

1 **courgette**, sliced

1 teaspoon **chopped chives**

naan bread, **crusty bread** or **rice** (see page 22) to serve

£ 0.91 /PERSON

2

2-3

PREP 15 MINS

COOK 60 MINS

1. Heat the oil in a saucepan. Add the onion, ginger, garlic and carrots. Cook for about 2 minutes until soft.

2. Add the peas, mustard, chilli, curry paste, tomato purée, tinned tomatoes, water and crumbled stock cubes. Bring to the boil and season well. Turn the heat down and simmer for about 40 minutes.

3. Add the squash and the courgette. Simmer for a further 10 minutes until the squash is tender. Stir the chives in, right at the end. Season well with salt and pepper.

4. Serve with naan bread, crusty bread or rice (see page 22).

Cannellini Bean Casserole

Eat it on its own, or with baked potatoes, rice or crusty bread. You can vary the beans used and add other vegetables if you wish. They will need to be quick-cook vegetables, such as mushrooms, or courgettes, not root vegetables.

£0.83 /PERSON

1

2

PREP
10 MINS

COOK
15 MINS

1 tablespoon **oil** to fry

3 small **shallots** (very small onions), sliced

1 clove **garlic**, chopped

1 stick **celery**, chopped

3 medium **tomatoes**, cut into chunks

½ mug **water** + 1 **vegetable stock cube**

400g tin **cannellini beans**, rinsed and drained

1 dessertspoon **tomato purée**

½ teaspoon **Tobasco sauce**, more if you like things spicy

1. Heat the oil in a saucepan and fry the shallots, garlic and celery for 2 minutes. Add the tomatoes and cook for a further 2 minutes. Add the water and crumbled stock cube and cook for another 1 minute.

2. Add the beans, tomato purée and the Tobasco sauce. Bring to the boil. Turn the heat down and cook for 2–3 minutes to heat the beans through. Season well and serve.

Winter Warming Hot Pot

This is a good basic recipe. You can add and subtract vegetables as you have them to hand. You can also replace the Marmite with different flavourings: chilli, curry paste, mustard, etc. You need to have a good variety within the pot for it to taste good. Serve with crusty bread or baked potatoes. Reheats well the next day.

£0.75 /PERSON

1

2-3

PREP 10 MINS

COOK 20 MINS

1 small **onion**, chopped

1 **carrot**, peeled and chopped into small chunks

1 **parsnip**, peeled and chopped into small chunks

¼ **swede**, peeled and chopped into chunks

¼ **celeriac**, peeled and chopped into small chunks

1 **courgette**, sliced

2 sticks **celery**, sliced

400g tin **pinto beans** or **black-eyed beans**, drained and rinsed

1 mug **water** + 1 **vegetable stock cube**, crumbled

1 teaspoon **Marmite** or yeast extract

1. Heat a little oil in a saucepan and fry the vegetables until they begin to brown a little. Season with salt and pepper.

2. Add the rest of the ingredients. Bring to the boil and then turn down to simmer for 20 minutes. Check to see that the vegetables are all cooked.

Gardener's Pie

No need to bother with mashed potatoes. If you want to cook it with Quorn mince, add after the vegetables in stage 2. Cook for a few minutes, before adding the tomatoes, etc.

£0.79 /PERSON

2

2-3

PREP 15 MINS

COOK 25 MINS

1 tablespoon **oil** to fry

½ **onion**, chopped

1 small **carrot**, chopped

5 **mushrooms**, sliced

1 clove **garlic**, chopped

400g can **chopped tomatoes**

½ x 400ml can **black-eyed** or **cannellini beans**

2 teaspoons **HP sauce**, or ¼ teaspoon **Tobasco sauce**

1 **vegetable stock cube**, crumbled

1 teaspoon **basil**

1 teaspoon **sugar**

Topping

2 large **potatoes**, diced

2cm cube **butter**

½ mug grated **Cheddar cheese**

1. Preheat the oven to 180°C fan oven/200°C/Gas 6. Put the diced potatoes on to simmer for 10 minutes.

2. Heat the oil in a saucepan. Fry the onions, carrots, mushrooms and garlic. Allow them to brown a little. Add the tomatoes, beans, HP (or Tobasco sauce), stock cube, basil and sugar. Cook for 10 minutes until the vegetables are tender.

3. Drain the potatoes and return them back into the pan. Add the butter mix. The potatoes should go a bit 'raggy' round the edges.

4. Put the bean mixture in a casserole dish and top with the potatoes. Sprinkle the cheese on top and bake in the oven for 25 minutes until the cheese has browned.

Chilli Bean Stew, with Crusty Bread

Reheats well. You can, of course vary the beans.

1 tablespoon **oil** to fry

1 **onion**, sliced

1 clove **garlic**, finely chopped

½ **red pepper**, chopped

4–5 **mushrooms**, sliced

400g tin **chopped tomatoes**

1 **vegetable stock cube**

½ teaspoon **chilli flakes**

1 tablespoon **tomato purée**

1 teaspoon **sugar**

½ mug **water**

½ x 400g tin **aduki beans**, drained and rinsed

½ x 400g tin **black-eyed beans**, drained and rinsed

crusty bread to serve

£1.50 /PERSON

1

2

PREP 20 MINS

1. Heat the oil in a wok. Add the onions and garlic and fry for 2–3 minutes. Add the peppers and mushrooms and fry for a further 2 minutes.

2. Add the tomatoes, stock, chilli flakes, tomato purée, sugar, water and beans and season well. Bring to the boil and then simmer for 5 minutes.

date-night

Need to impress that special someone without slogging in the kitchen for hours? Try some of these 'scrummy' recipes.

Stuffed Aubergine

Aubergines are a good source of fibre and folic acid. Probably best bought June to September, when they are in season and a little cheaper.

1 large **aubergine**

oil

100g **feta cheese**

10 **olives**, chopped

100g **pine nuts**

3 pieces **sun-dried tomato**, chopped

½ mug **Parmesan-style cheese**

PREP
30 MINS

COOK
15 MINS

1. Preheat the oven to 200°C fan oven/220°C/Gas 7. Lightly grease a baking tray.

2. Cut the aubergine in half and brush with oil. Place in the oven, for 20–25 minutes until the flesh in the middle is soft enough to scoop out.

3. Meanwhile, mix together the feta, olives, pine nuts and sun-dried tomatoes. Season well.

4. Once the aubergines are cooked, scoop out the soft flesh from the middle and mix together with the cheese mixture. Place back in the aubergine shells. Sprinkle over with grated Parmesan.

5. Place back in the oven for 10–15 minutes until the cheese is brown.

6. Serve with some salad.

date-night **163**

...m and Brie Pasta

...little more expensive than the usual Cheddar, but ...t bit more special. Any excess will make a delicious ...some salad to it.

...spoon **oil**

3 **spring onions**, chopped

2 cloves of **garlic**, finely chopped

8 medium **mushrooms**, sliced

½ **vegetable stock cube** crumbled into 4 tablespoons **water**

5 pieces **sun-dried tomatoes**, sliced

1 dessertspoon **wholegrain mustard**

4 tablespoons **double cream**

125g pack of **Brie**, cut into slices

1. Put the pasta on to cook (see page 23).
2. Heat oil in a frying pan. Fry the spring onions, garlic and mushrooms until the mushrooms are soft.
3. Add the stock cube and water and simmer, uncovered, until almost all the stock has reduced.
4. Add the tomatoes, mustard, cream and cheese. Cook until the Brie has melted.
5. Stir in the cooked, drained pasta.
6. Season well and serve.

Pasta with Onions and Green Beans

The preparation time here is a bit lengthy, but not too difficult. The final result is a lovely sweet-and-sour flavour not usually associated with pasta dishes.

£1.59 /PERSON

3

1

PREP 30 MINS

½ x 200g pack **green beans**

1 tablespoon **oil** to fry

1 **red onion**, sliced

1 **garlic clove**, chopped

2 tablespoons **water**

1 tablespoon **raisins**

2 tablespoons **sugar**

2 tablespoons **red** or **white wine vinegar**

¼ x 200g pack of **spinach**

one portion of **tagliatelle** (see page 23)

1. Put the beans in boiling water and simmer for 5 minutes. Drain and return to the pan.

2. Put the pasta on to cook (see page 23).

3. Heat a little oil in a frying pan and fry the onions and garlic for about 6–8 minutes. Stir frequently. They should be soft and quite brown.

4. Add the water, raisins, sugar and vinegar and cook for 2–3 minutes.

5. Add the spinach and cook until it wilts. Add the green beans.

6. Drain the pasta and put on a plate. Top with the onions and beans.

Mushroom Stroganoff

£1.53 /PERSON

1

2

PREP
15 MINS

It is worth buying different varieties of mushroom to use in this dish. Shitake mushrooms have a great flavour and are not too expensive.

1 tablespoon **oil** to fry

1 small **onion**, chopped finely

2 **celery sticks**, sliced finely

12 medium **mushrooms**, sliced

1 dessertspoon **flour**

1 **vegetable stock cube**,

1 tablespoon **wholegrain mustard**, dissolved in ½ mug **water**

1 dessertspoon **chives**

2 tablespoons **soured cream**

rice to serve (see page 22)

1. Cook the rice.

2. Put the oil in the pan and fry the onions and celery until they begin to soften. Add a little more oil to the pan, add the mushrooms and cook for 1 minute.

3. Add the flour to the pan. Mix together and then add the crumbled stock cube, mustard and water. Bring to the boil, then turn down the heat and simmer, uncovered, for 1 minute.

4. Take off the heat and add the soured cream and the chives. Season with salt and pepper.

5. Serve with rice.

Creamy Parmesan-Style Pasta

If you wish, you could add mushrooms to this recipe.

2 mugs of **pasta**

3cm cube **butter**

5 **spring onions**, chopped

1 small clove **garlic**, finely chopped

100g pack **pine nuts**

½ mug **frozen peas**

1 mug **double cream**

½ teaspoon **nutmeg**

1 mug **grated Parmesan-style cheese**

£2.29 /PERSON

2

2

PREP 25 MINS

1. Put the pasta on to cook (see page 23). Drain and leave in the pan.

2. Heat the butter in a frying pan and add the onions, garlic and pine nuts. Fry until the onions begin to soften and brown.

3. Add the frozen peas to the pan and stir.

4. Add the cream and the nutmeg and bring to the boil. Stir in the grated Parmesan and drained pasta. Take off the heat immediately. Season well with salt and pepper.

Sweet and Sour Quorn

You can use this sweet and sour sauce with other recipes.

Sweet and Sour Sauce

1 tablespoon **sugar**

1 dessertspoon **cornflour**

2 tablespoons **wine vinegar**

1 tablespoon **soy sauce**

1 tablespoon **tomato purée**

³/₄ mug **water**

rice to serve (see page 22)

1 tablespoon **oil** to fry

¹/₂ **onion**, sliced

1 clove **garlic**, finely chopped

¹/₂ **red pepper**, sliced

¹/₂ x 300g packet of **chicken-style Quorn pieces**

¹/₄ x 250g pack **mangetout**, each cut into 4

227g tin **pineapple chunks**, drained

1. Mix the sauce ingredients together. Leave to one side until needed.

2. Heat the oil in a wok or large saucepan. Add the onions, garlic, peppers and Quorn. Fry until the onions begin to soften.

3. Add the mangetout and pineapple chunks to the pan. Fry for 1 minute.

4. Add the sauce and bring to the boil.

5. Turn down to simmer for 1 minute.

6. Serve with rice (see page 22).

Peppers Stuffed with Feta & Pine Nuts

£2.10 /PERSON

3

2

PREP
10 MINS

COOK
25 MINS

Cut some of the lumpy bits off the bottoms of the peppers so they 'stand up' on the tray.

2 large **red** or **yellow peppers**

¼ mug **couscous** + ½ mug boiling **water** + 1 **vegetable stock cube**

1 tablespoon **olive oil**

3 **spring onions**, chopped

4 **ready-to-eat dried apricots**, chopped

200g **feta cheese**, crumbled

1 medium **tomato**, chopped finely

½ x 100g pack **pine nuts**

1 tablespoon freshly chopped **basil**

---

1. Preheat the oven to 180°C fan oven/200°C/Gas 6. Grease a baking tray.

2. Cut the tops off each pepper and scoop out the seeds and the veins. Stand on the tray.

3. Put the couscous in a bowl with the boiling water and stock cube. Cover with a plate and leave to soak for 4–5 minutes. All the water should have been absorbed.

4. Add the rest of the ingredients and mix together. Season with pepper. The feta is quite salty, so don't add more.

5. Fill the peppers with the mixture. Put them on the baking tray and place them in the oven for 25 minutes. The tops should be nicely browned.

6. Serve with salad, or mini roast potatoes.

Feta Caesar Salad

If you leave the peeled avocado uncovered, it will soon turn brown. Once the dressing is poured over it, it is OK.

1 tablespoon **oil** to fry

1 slice **wholemeal bread**

1 small **cos lettuce**, cut into strips

4 **spring onions**, cut into long strips

1 **avocado**, peeled and cut into thin wedges

5cm piece of **cucumber**, cut into strips

½ x 200g pack **feta cheese**

½ mug grated **Parmesan-style cheese**

Dressing

2 tablespoons **olive oil**

1 tablespoon **mayo**

1 teaspoon **wholegrain mustard**

1 teaspoon **sugar**

salt and **pepper**

£1.19 /PERSON

1

2

PREP 20 MINS

1. Prepare the dressing by mixing the ingredients together.

2. Heat a little oil in a frying pan and fry the slice of bread until it is browned on both sides. Cut into cubes.

3. Mix together the lettuce, spring onions, avocado, fried bread and cucumber. Add the dressing and mix well.

4. Crumble the feta on top of the salad and sprinkle the Parmesan over. Ready to eat!

cakes & cookies

Looking for some comforting nibbles?
Try a few of these and share them with friends.

cakes &
cookies

Dream Bars

You can vary the actual nuts and the seeds you use, just keep to the same amounts. Be careful to stick to the timing at stage 3, otherwise the bars will not set.

1 mug ready-to-eat **dried apricots**, chopped

³/₄ mug **desiccated coconut**

¹/₂ x 100g pack of **toasted, flaked almonds**

¹/₂ x 100g pack of **sunflower** or

pumpkin seeds

3¹/₂ mugs **Rice Krispies**

100g **butter** (measure using packet)

²/₃ mug **brown sugar**

2 rounded tablespoons **golden syrup**

£0.16 /EACH

3

20

PREP 15 MINS

COOL 1 HOUR

1. Grease and line a baking tray.

2. Put the apricots, coconut, nuts, pumpkin seeds and Rice Krispies in a bowl. Mix together.

3. Put the butter, sugar and syrup in a pan and melt. Simmer briskly for 1¹/₂ minutes. The sugar should all be dissolved and the mixture will be like toffee. The sugar is very hot at this point, so take care.

4. Pour immediately into the dry ingredients in the bowl. Mix fairly quickly and thoroughly, making sure that there are no dry patches.

5. Turn out into the baking tray. Press down so that it sticks together and spreads out. Leave for about 1 hour to set and cool. Cut into pieces and eat.

Muffins

Muffins are really quick and easy to make and there are many variations. There are a few listed here.

3 mugs **self-raising flour**

1 mug **brown sugar** (you can use white)

2 **eggs**, slightly beaten

1½ mugs **milk**

¾ mug **vegetable oil**

£0.10 /MUFFIN

2

12

PREP 15 MINS

COOK 20 MINS

1. Preheat the oven to 180°C fan oven/200°C/Gas 6.

2. Mix the flour and sugar in a bowl.

3. Add the eggs, milk and oil into the bowl. Stir together. The mixture will be a bit lumpy, but do not overmix.

4. If you have cake tins, use them and put paper cake cases in each hole. If you do not have cake tins, put double paper cake cases for each muffin on your baking tray. This will help the cases hold their shape. Spoon the mixture into each case.

5. Bake in the oven for 20 minutes. If you use the larger muffin cases, you will need to bake them for 25 minutes. They should be a little brown and spring back when gently pressed.

Variations

Once you have the hang of these variations, you can experiment with your own varieties. Don't put anything too wet into the ingredients and don't add more liquid. If you want to add something very wet, then reduce the quantity of milk by a proportional amount.

Summers fruit

Just add $1/2$ x 500g bag of frozen, defrosted and drained, **summer fruit** to the wet ingredients. Bake as usual.

Apple

Add 2 cooking or **eating apples**, cored and chopped up, + 1 teaspoon **cinnamon** to the dry ingredients.

Dates

Add 1 mug chopped **dates**, 2 teaspoons **ground ginger**, $1/2$ teaspoon **cinnamon** and the grated rind of an **orange** to the dry ingredients.

Nuts

Add 1 mug chopped **pecan nuts** + 2 teaspoons **instant coffee grains** to the dry ingredients.

White chocolate and berry

Add 100g pack of **white chocolate chips** and $1/2$ x 500g pack frozen **fruits of the forest** along with the wet ingredients.

Apricot and marmalade

Replace $1/2$ mug **flour** with $1/2$ mug **muesli**. Add 100g ready-to-eat **apricots**, chopped and the grated rind of 1 **orange** to the dry ingredients. When the mixture is in the cases, but before it goes into the oven, drop 1 teaspoon of **marmalade** into the centre of each muffin. Bake as usual.

Honey and oats

Replace $1/2$ mug of flour with $1/2$ mug **oats** and add $1/2$ teaspoon **cinnamon** and $1/2$ mug **raisins** to the dry ingredients and 2 tablespoons of honey to the wet ingredients.

Banana and nut

Squash 2 large **bananas** and add when the mixture is wet, together with $1/2$ mug **chopped nuts**.

Cranberry and poppy seed

Add 4 teaspoons **poppy seeds** to the dry ingredients and a 140g pack of **dried cranberries** to the wet ingredients.

Chocolate chip muffins

Add two 100g packets of **chocolate chips**. Two different varieties work well; for example, white and milk, or plain chocolate. If you want double choc chip muffins, instead of the 3 mugs of flour, use $2^2/_3$ mugs of **flour** and $1/3$ mug of **drinking chocolate**.

Cashew Nut Cookies

Creamed coconut is usually found in the 'Oriental foods' section at the supermarket.

150g softened **butter** (measure using packet)

$^2/_3$ mug **brown sugar**

1 **egg**

200g pack **cashew nuts**, roughly chopped

½ x 200g packet of **creamed coconut**, grated

1 mug **self-raising flour**

1 dessertspoon ground **ginger** (optional)

£0.25 /EACH

3

16

PREP 20 MINS

COOK 15 MINS

1. Preheat the oven to 180°C fan oven/200°C/Gas 6.

2. Cream the butter and sugar in a bowl and beat in the egg.

3. Add the rest of the ingredients and mix well.

4. Tip out onto a floured surface and squash into a long sausage. The dough is quite sticky. Cut into 16 and make each shape into a round, but do not squash too flat.

5. Place on a greased baking tray (you can cook in batches if you only have one tray). Bake in the oven for 15 minutes. The cookies should be golden brown.

Nutty Honey Cake

This will keep for a week, if kept in a tin or a sealed bag. Good way of using up over-ripe bananas.

1 large **banana**

2 **eggs**

3 tablespoons **honey**

1/3 x 250g pack stoned **dates**, chopped

3/4 mug **brown sugar**

50g pack of **pecan nuts** (other varieties are OK)

150g **butter** (measure using packet)

1 1/2 mugs **self-raising flour**

1/2 teaspoon **cinnamon**

1. Preheat the oven to 160°C fan oven/180°C/Gas 4. Grease and line a loaf tin.
2. Peel and mash the banana in a fairly large bowl.
3. Add the eggs and beat together. Add the honey, dates, sugar and the nuts. Mix well.
4. Melt the butter over a low heat in a pan, then stir into the mixture in the bowl.
5. Add the flour and the cinnamon to the bowl. Mix well, but do not beat vigorously. Pour into the loaf tin.
6. Cook in the oven for 1 hour. The cake should spring back when pressed gently on the top.

£0.26 /PERSON

2

12

PREP 15 MINS

COOK 60 MINS

Cherry Cookies

Don't eat straight away, as the cherries are very hot!

250g block **butter**, softened

2/3 mug **sugar**

200g pack of **cochineal-free glacé cherries**

2 tablespoons **mixed fruit** or **raisins**

1 mug **self-raising flour**

2 mugs **oats**

1. Preheat the oven to 160°C fan oven/180°C/Gas 4.

2. Cream the softened butter and sugar together in a bowl until they are light and fluffy.

3. Stir in the whole cherries, flour, fruit and oats. It seems at first as though it will not mix in, but it does.

4. Tip the mixture onto a floured surface and squeeze together. Divide into approx. 18 pieces and roll into balls. Grease a baking tray and squash the balls down, so they are just over 2cm thick. They will spread a bit when you cook them, so place them apart. Cook in the oven for 15–20 minutes. They should go golden brown.

Date and Banana Swirls

Much like the Cherry cookies on the opposite page, don't eat them straight away, as the jam and bananas will be very hot!

320g **ready-rolled puff pastry**

2 tablespoons **apricot jam**

4 **dates**, chopped

2 **bananas**, chopped

1 beaten **egg**

£0.22 /EACH

3

9

PREP 20 MINS

COOK 25 MINS

1. Preheat the oven to 200ºC fan oven/220ºC/ gas7.
2. Grease a large baking tray.
3. Unroll the pastry onto a floured surface. Spread the jam over evenly. Spread the chopped dates evenly.
4. Squish the bananas as you distribute them evenly over the pastry.
5. Roll up from the longest side of the pastry.
6. Cut into 3cm pieces and transfer onto the tray.
7. Brush with the beaten egg and bake in the oven for 25 minutes. The swirls should have puffed up and be golden brown.

Orange Chocolate Cake

You will need to buy a cake tin if you want to make this one. It would make a great birthday cake for someone.

100g **dark chocolate**

3 **oranges**

3 **eggs**

3/4 mug **sunflower oil**

1¼ mugs **caster sugar**

1½ mugs **self-raising flour**

3 tablespoons **cocoa**

Topping

200g **dark chocolate**

1 mug **double cream**

£0.36 /SLICE

4

16

PREP 20 MINS

COOK 55 MINS

1. Preheat the oven to 160°C fan oven/180°C/Gas 5. Grease a 23cm cake tin and put a circle of greaseproof paper in the bottom.

2. Break up 100g of chocolate and melt, gently, in a bowl over a saucepan of simmering water. Once melted, take off the heat.

3. Grate the rind from one of the oranges and place in a mixing bowl. Cut the peel off all 3 oranges and put the flesh in the bowl with the grated rind. Whizz with the blender.

4. Beat the eggs and add to the bowl, with the oil and sugar. Beat well.

5. By now the chocolate should have cooled a little, so add to the bowl and mix well.

6. Add the flour and the cocoa. Mix well, but do not beat. The mixture will be very wet, don't worry! Pour the mixture into the cake tin and bake in the oven for 50–55 minutes. The cake should spring back when gently pressed.

7. To make the topping, put the cream in a saucepan and bring to the boil. Immediately take off the heat. Break up 200g chocolate, add to the cream and stir until it melts. Leave to cool and it will start to set. Once the cake has cooled and the topping has begun to set, spread it over the top. Serve on its own, or with cream.

For something a bit more colourful, check out a cake Joy made with Bella, her grandaughter, at noshbooks.com/bella-cake

Lime and Coconut Drizzle Cake

£0.18 /EACH

★ 3

12

PREP 15 MINS

COOK 25 MINS

150g softened **butter** (measure using packet)

½ mug **caster sugar**

2 **eggs**

zest of 2 **limes**

¾ mug **self-raising flour**

½ teaspoon **baking powder**

¼ mug **desiccated coconut**

1 teaspoon **vanilla essence**

2 tablespoons **water**

Topping

4 tablespoons **granulated sugar**

juice of 2 **limes**

1. Preheat the oven to 180ºC fan oven/200ºC/gas 6. Grease and line an 18cm cake tin.

2. Beat together the butter and sugar.

3. Add the eggs one at a time, beating well between each addition

4. Add the lime zest and beat.

5. Add the rest of the ingredients and fold in gently.

6. Turn into the cake tin and smooth out.

7. Bake for 25 minutes. The top should be lightly browned and the cake should spring back when lightly pressed.

8. Mix together the sugar and lime juice. Spread evenly over the warm cake. Leave to cool before taking out of the tin and slicing.

Oat Crunchies

If you only have one baking tray, it is OK to leave half the mixture standing while you cook the first half.

1 mug **rolled oats**

1 mug **desiccated coconut**

1 mug **self-raising flour**

1/2 mug **sugar**

100g **butter** (measure using packet)

1 heaped tablespoon **golden syrup**

3 tablespoons **water**

£0.06 /EACH

2

24

PREP 15 MINS

COOK 12 MINS

1. Preheat the oven to 180°C fan oven/200°C/Gas 6.

2. Put all the dry ingredients in a bowl.

3. Melt the butter in a pan on a low heat. Add the syrup and the water and stir. Pour into the dry ingredients and mix well.

4. Grease a baking tray. Take about a tablespoon of the mixture at a time, squeeze into a ball and place on the baking tray. Squash down gently. Place them a little apart, since they will spread as they cook. Put about 8–12 on the tray.

5. Bake for 10–12 minutes until golden brown.

White Chocolate Cherry Fudge

500g **white chocolate**
397g **condensed milk**
1/3 mug **icing sugar**
1 mug **desiccated coconut**

200g **vegetarian glacé cherries**, chopped
1/2 mug **pistachios**, chopped

£0.27 /EACH

2

24

PREP 20 MINS

FRIDGE 4 HRS

1. Line a traybake tin with greaseproof paper.
2. Gently melt the white chocolate in a large bowl over a pan of gently simmering water.
3. Take the bowl off the heat and beat in the condensed milk and the sugar.
4. Stir in the coconut, cherries and pistachios.
5. Pour into the lined traybake tin and smooth out evenly.
6. Leave in the fridge for 4 hours.
7. Cut into 2cm cubes.
8. Store in the fridge.

Orange and Lemon Buns

170g softened **butter**, measure using packet

¾ mug **caster sugar**

3 **eggs**

zest of an **orange**

zest of a **lemon**

1 ¼ mugs **self-raising flour**

2 tablespoons cold **water**

200g **icing sugar**

juice of a **lemon**

juice of an **orange**

vegetarian safe food colouring (see page 14)

15 **bun cases**

1. Preheat the oven to 180ºC fan oven/200ºC/gas 6.

2. Put 12 bun cases into bun tins.

3. Beat the butter and sugar together until light and fluffy.

4. Add the eggs, one at a time, beating well between each addition.

5. Add the orange and lemon zest and beat together.

6. Gently fold in the flour and then add the water. Mix gently.

7. Divide between the bun cases and bake in the oven for 20–25 minutes. The cakes should be golden brown and spring back when lightly pressed.

8. Make up the icing. Divide the icing sugar between 2 small bowls. Add lemon juice to one and orange to the other, just enough to make a thick paste. Add the food colouring to make the lemon yellow and the orange orange-coloured.

9. Once the cakes are cooled, put the icing into freezer bags, snip off one corner and squeeze the icing through the holes and over the buns. No need to be too careful doing this, see photo!

Chocolate Truffles

These make good gifts if you wrap them prettily. Keep them in the fridge.

200g block of **dark chocolate**

75g **butter** (measure using packet)

⅓ mug **icing sugar**

2 teaspoons **vanilla extract**

1 mug **ground almonds**,

grated **chocolate**, drinking chocolate, chocolate bits, or **icing sugar**, to roll the truffles in.

£0.17 /EACH

3

24

PREP 15 MINS

1. Melt the chocolate and butter in a bowl over a saucepan of simmering water. Take off the heat.

2. Add the icing sugar, vanilla extract and the ground almonds. Mix well and leave to cool slightly.

3. Turn out onto a board and cut into 24 pieces. Roll them into balls and then roll in the grated chocolate, drinking chocolate, chocolate bits or icing sugar. Leave in the fridge until required.

Pecan and Chocolate Squares

Desiccated coconut is usually found in the 'baking section' at the supermarket.

2 mugs **rolled oats**

3 tablespoons **desiccated coconut**

125g **butter** (measure using packet)

½ mug **brown sugar**

3 tablespoons **golden syrup**

100g pack **pecan** or other nuts (or a mixture), chopped roughly

100g packet of **chocolate chips**

£0.20 /EACH

2

18

PREP 15 MINS

COOK 25 MINS

1. Preheat the oven to 160°C fan oven/180°C/Gas 5.

2. Put the oats and coconut in a bowl.

3. Put the butter, sugar and syrup in a pan. Heat gently until the sugar has melted. Stir into the oat mixture. Mix well.

4. Press into a greased baking tray. Press the nuts and the chocolate into the top.

5. Cook in the oven for 20–25 minutes until golden brown. Allow to cool in the tray and then cut into pieces.

Chocolate Krispy Munchies

You can ring the changes with this recipe, try cornflakes instead of the Rice Krispies. Also try other chocolate bars, or Maltesers, instead of the Twix bars. These make great gifts and they do need to be kept in the fridge.

250g bar of **dark chocolate**

1 tablespoon **golden syrup**

100g **butter** (measure using packet)

½ mug **soft brown sugar**

3 mugs **Rice Krispies**

300g of **Twix bars**

£ 0.14 /EACH

1

30

PREP 25 MINS

COOL 2 HRS

---

1. Line an 18cm x 27cm baking tray with greaseproof paper.

2. Put the chocolate, syrup, butter and sugar into a bowl and place over a pan of simmering water. Melt gently, stirring occasionally. Leave to cool a little.

3. Cut the Twix bars into chunks and place in a large bowl with the Rice Krispies.

4. Quickly stir in the chocolate mixture. Pour into the prepared tray and press down.

5. Leave in the fridge for a couple of hours and then cut into squares.

For more cakes and cookies go to noshbooks.com/cookies

desserts

Think that making desserts is too difficult, but you have some friends around? Try some of these. Just don't think about the calories!

desserts

Tiramisu

This version is a bit of a cheat, but still tastes fantastic and is really easy.

1 tablespoon **instant coffee**
+ 3 tablespoons **hot water**

2–3 tablespoons **brandy** or **rum**

½ x 175g pack **sponge fingers**

500g **mascarpone** cheese

425g tin **custard**

2 tablespoons **icing sugar**

cocoa powder to finish

£0.84 /PERSON

3

4-6

PREP 20 MINS

COOL 1 HOUR

1. Mix the coffee with the water and alcohol. Dip the sponge fingers in the liquid and use them to line the bottom of a bowl. If you do not have a glass bowl, a casserole dish will do.

2. Soften the mascarpone cheese with a spoon and mix in the custard and sugar until it is smooth. Pile on top of the sponge fingers.

3. Leave to set for about 1 hour and then sprinkle cocoa on the top (see photo).

Baked Apples

Easy way to make a dessert for one person. Serve with a little cream, yogurt, crème fraîche, or custard.

1 pink lady **apple**

1 tablespoon **brown sugar**

2 tablespoons **sultanas** or **raisins**

a little **butter**

1 dessertspoon **honey**

£0.37 /PERSON

1

1

PREP 10 MINS

COOK 30 MINS

1. Preheat the oven to 180°C fan oven/200°C/Gas 6.

2. Wash the apple and cut out the core from the centre, leaving the apple whole. Score a horizontal line around the centre of the apple (see photo). This stops the skin from bursting.

3. Mix together the sugar and the fruit. Stuff it into the space where the core was. Place on an ovenproof dish, a casserole dish is fine. Place small pieces of butter around the top of the apple. Spoon the honey over the apple. If you have spare fruit and sugar, sprinkle around the bottom of the apple and it will turn into toffee as the apple cooks.

4. Bake in the oven for 25–30 minutes.

Apple Crumble

You can add many fruits, e.g. blackberries, rhubarb, plums. Cook the fruit in the same way as the apples, taking care not to overcook them and turn them into pulp.

£0.20 /PERSON

2

4

PREP 15 MINS

COOK 25 MINS

2 large **cooking apples**
½ mug **water**
½ mug **brown sugar** (white is OK)
½ teaspoon **mixed spice** (optional)

Topping
1 mug **plain flour**
100g **butter** (measure using packet)
½ mug **sugar**

1. Preheat the oven to 180°C fan oven/200°C/Gas 6.

2. Peel the apples and remove the core. Cut into chunks and place in a pan with ½ mug of water. Bring to the boil and allow to cook for 3–4 minutes. The apples will begin to go fluffy round the edges and soften. When they do, add the sugar and the mixed spice (if you add the sugar at the beginning, the apples will stay hard). Stir in the sugar and pour into the bottom of an ovenproof dish. Set the dish aside while you make the topping.

3. Put the flour and butter in a bowl. With your fingers and thumbs, rub the butter into the flour until it looks a bit like breadcrumbs. Add the sugar and mix. Gently spoon on top of the apple mixture and spread evenly. Press down with a fork.

4. Cook in the oven for 20-25 minutes. Serve warm with custard, ice cream, or cream.

Eton Mess

200ml **double cream**

2 **ready-made meringue nests**

150g **strawberries**, chopped

2 **Mars bars**, chopped up

1. Beat the cream in a large bowl, until it is thick.
2. Break up the meringues into large-ish chunks and add to the cream, along with the strawberries. Gently mix together.
3. Spoon into bowls and sprinkle the chopped Mars bars over the top.

Bread and Butter Pud

This is a good way to use up any leftover bread. You can use any type of bread and can add things like chopped up apricots, spoonfuls of marmalade, honey and dried fruits.

3 slices of **bread**

butter to spread

2 tablespoons **sugar**

2 tablespoons **raisins**

3 **eggs**

1 mug **milk**

¼ teaspoon **cinnamon** (optional)

£0.28 /PERSON

1

2-3

PREP 10 MINS

COOK 25 MINS

1. Preheat the oven to 180°C fan oven/200°C/Gas 6.
2. Spread the bread with butter and cut each slice into 4 triangular pieces. Arrange them in a casserole dish.
3. Sprinkle the sugar and the raisins around the bread.
4. Beat the eggs and add the milk and cinnamon. Pour over the bread.
5. Cook in the oven for 20–25 minutes. The bread should be browned and the eggs set.

Fruity Rice

You can make this with most fruits. Here, I have used fruits of the forest, since they are amongst the most convenient fruits. You can used tinned fruits; frozen are more healthy, because tinned fruits usually have a lot of sugar added. Fresh fruit is, of course, the best. Strawberries, blackberries, blackcurrants, blueberries and raspberries will work very well.

425g tin **rice pudding**

½ x 500g pack of frozen **fruits of the forest**, defrosted

1 teaspoon **vanilla extract**

£0.75 /PERSON

1

2

PREP 5 MINS

1. Place the rice pudding in a bowl and stir in the vanilla extract.

2. Once the fruit is defrosted, place about 1 tablespoon in the bottom of each dish. If you have glass dishes, that's great, otherwise use cereal bowls. Put half the rice in each bowl. Add more fruit on the top. Serve. Dead easy!

Fruit Fool

You can use other fruits to vary this very easy recipe. Suggested fruits: fruits of the forest, raspberries, mangoes, peaches, blueberries and blackberries. It works best with fresh fruit.

£0.62 /PERSON

1

2

PREP 15 MINS

4 **sponge fingers**

2 tablespoons **orange juice**, or the juice of an orange. You can vary this according to the fruits you use.

2 **kiwi** fruits

6 large **strawberries**

425g pot of fresh **custard**

½ x 450g pot of **Greek yogurt** with honey, or any other flavoured yogurt

1. Break the sponge fingers in two. Divide them between 2 bowls. You could use big wine glasses. Pour the orange juice over the sponges.

2. Peel the kiwi fruits and slice thinly. Wash and slice the strawberries.

3. Arrange the fruits, custard and yogurt in 'areas', not so much layers (see photo). Make it look as pretty as possible.

Pancakes

Pancakes are good fun when you have friends around. Just make sure others are helping in the cooking process. Tossing them is always fun, but catching them is not guaranteed!

£0.67 /PANCAKE

2

2

PREP 25 MINS

Pancakes

2 **eggs**

6 tablespoons **self-raising flour**

milk (see below)

Trex or white **Flora** to fry (you can use oil but a lard type is best)

Serving suggestions

Strawberries

Double cream, whipped

chocolate sauce. To make your own go to:
noshbooks.com/chocolate-sauce

1. Beat the eggs and flour together in a bowl or jug. Gradually add enough milk until the mixture is as thin as single cream, i.e. quite thin, but not as thin as milk.

2. Heat a little Trex in a frying pan. When the fat begins to smoke a little, pour approximately 2 tablespoons of the mixture into the pan. Tip the pan around, so that the mixture spreads over the surface of the pan. Let the mixture cook for about 1 minute.

3. Gently lift the edge of the pancake to see if it is browned. Once browned, turn the pancake with a slotted turner, or toss and then cook the other side. For serving suggestions see above.

Berry Trifle

Very easy to make. Be careful not to beat the cream too much, or you will have made yourself some butter!

1 **chocolate Swiss roll**

500g pack of **frozen summer fruits** or **raspberries**, defrosted

2 tablespoons **icing sugar**

½ mug **sherry** or other alcohol (optional)

425g can of **custard**

1 mug or ½ pint of **double cream**

grated **chocolate** or a broken-up **flake** for the topping

£0.82 /PERSON

2

4-6

PREP 20 MINS

COOL 60 MINS

1. Cut about 6–8 slices of the Swiss roll and arrange them on the bottom of a dish.

2. Mix the icing sugar with the fruit and distribute evenly over the Swiss roll. Allow the juices to seep into the Swiss roll.

3. Pour over the sherry.

4. Pour the custard over the fruit.

5. Beat the cream until it is thick. Carefully spread over the top.

6. Sprinkle the chocolate over the top and leave in the fridge to cool for 1 hour.

Menu 1

Monday Beanburgers p63

Tuesday other beanburger

Wednesday Tomato and Lentil Soup p56

Thursday Quorn Curry p67

Friday rest of Quorn Curry

Saturday ½ quantity Risotto p78

Sunday Leek and Potato Frittata p73

check cupboards for:
- butter
- pickles (for burger)
- red lentils
- Marmite
- Madras curry paste
- raisins
- stock cubes
- oil
- rice
- garlic
- basil
- sugar
- tomato purée
- white wine vinegar

Here you cook 5 times in the week and share 1 meal. The approximate cost would be £18.

Shopping List
- bread
- milk
- cereal
- sandwich fillers
- garlic
- 6 onions
- 1 carrot
- 1 large potato
- 3 small leeks
- 1 sweet potato
- 2 mushrooms
- 1 courgette
- salad (for Sunday)
- 12 eggs (leaves 5 spare for sandwiches)
- 200g pack feta cheese
- 200g pack Cheddar cheese
- 100g pack pine nuts
- 3 x 400g tins chopped tomatoes
- 350g packet frozen chicken style Quorn
- 750g pack frozen broad beans
- 1 bag plain crisps
- 2 bread buns
- Arborio risotto rice

Shopping List

- 2 carrots
- 3 potatoes
- 2 sweet potatoes
- 5 spring onions
- 3 courgettes
- 4 cherry tomatoes
- 3 onions
- 5 mushrooms
- 1 baby aubergine
- 1 red pepper
- 400g tin black-eyed beans
- 250g pack of Cheddar cheese
- 2 x 400g tins chopped tomatoes
- 130g tin sweetcorn
- 6 eggs (5 spare for sandwiches)
- 1 tin cannellini beans
- milk
- bread
- cereal
- sandwich fillers
- couscous
- self-raising flour

Menu 2

<u>Monday</u>   Roast Sweet Potatoes with Couscous p74

<u>Tuesday</u>   Rest of Sweet Potato

<u>Wednesday</u> Veggie Bake p100

<u>Thursday</u>   Rest of Veggie Bake

<u>Friday</u>   Gardener's Pie p160

<u>Saturday</u> rest of Gardner's Pie

<u>Sunday</u>   Corn cakes and Ratatouille - share p98

check cupboards for:

- oil
- tomato purée
- balsamic vinegar
- dried chives
- garlic
- Tobasco or HP sauce
- veg stock
- dried basil
- dried rosemary
- sugar
- butter

This week you cook 4 times and share one. It should cost approximately £17. The shopping list assumes cereal for breakfast and sandwiches for lunch each day.

Menu 3

Monday   Baked Veggie Patties p66

Tuesday   eat rest Baked Veggie Patties

Wednesday   Spag Bol p108

Thursday   eat rest of Spag Bol

Friday   Thai Coconut Curry p53

Saturday   eat rest of Thai Coconut Curry

Sunday   Red Chilli Tofu p125 - share

check cupboards for:

- veg stock
- oil
- chilli flakes
- oregano
- red lentils
- spaghetti
- garlic
- dried chives
- dried basil
- soy sauce
- flour
- tomato purée
- rice
- Thai red curry paste

Shopping List

- 1 sweet potato
- 2 potatoes
- 5 onions
- 3 carrots
- 1 courgette
- celery
- red pepper
- 250g green beans
- 1 small broccoli
- 6 eggs (leaves 5 spare for sandwiches)
- small carton of double cream
- small piece Parmesan-style cheese
- 2 x 400g tins chopped tomatoes
- 400g can of coconut milk
- 200g pack of Cheddar cheese (plenty spare for sandwiches)
- 375g pack tofu
- bread
- milk
- cereal
- sandwich fillings

Here you cook 4 times and share one meal. Assuming that you eat cereal for breakfast and sandwiches for lunch, should cost approximately £17.

Shopping List

- 4 onions
- 2 tomatoes
- 200g pack fresh spinach
- 1 courgette
- 1 carrot
- salad for Saturday
- 6 eggs
- bread
- milk
- cereal
- sandwich fillings
- 400g tin chickpeas
- 400g tin tomatoes
- frozen peas
- 150g pack Cheddar cheese
- small carton of Greek yogurt
- 100g pack pine nuts
- 200g pack chopped mixed nuts
- natural yogurt

Menu 4

Monday French Onion Soup p55

Tuesday Rest of French Onion Soup

Wednesday Egg Curry p64

Thursday Korma Rice p76

Friday rest of Korma Rice

Saturday Nut and Courgette Slice p116

Sunday rest of Nut and Courgette Slice

check cupboards for:

- oil
- Marmite
- curry paste
- rice
- mango chutney
- garlic
- raisins
- stock cubes

Here you cook 4 times and share once. It should cost you about £17, assuming cereal for breakfast and sandwiches at lunch.

index

A

all you need 6
apple and bean salad 60
apple and squash curry 86
apple crumble 193
aubergine and coconut curry 87
avocado salsa 145

B

baked apples 192
baked eggs 131
baked patties with chilli sauce 66
banana, honey and yogurt 34
basic risotto 78
basic stir-fry 80
bean burgers 63
bean risotto 79
beans
    bean burgers 63
    beans on toast with egg on top 28
    cannellini bean casserole 158
    cannellini bean spaghetti 44
    chilli bean stew, with crusty bread 161
    korma beans with naan 107
    pasta with onions and green beans 165
    quorn chilli with aduki beans 85
    spinach, bean and potato bake 112
beans on toast with egg on top 28
bean sprouts and vegetables 82
berry trifle 199
big wraps 148
biryani with yogurt and cashews 69
boiled eggs 30
boiling veggies 20
bolognese 108
bread
    beans on toast with egg on top 28
    cheese on toast 28
    interesting sandwiches 26
    stuff on toast 28
    welsh rarebit 28
bread and butter pud 195
bubble and squeak 91
bulgar wheat salad 117

C

cake
    lime and coconut drizzle cake 182
cakes and cookies
    cashew nut cookies 176
    chocolate krispie munchies 188
    chocolate truffles 186
    dream bars 173
    muffins 174
    nutty fruit bars 179
    nutty honey cake 177
    oat crunchies 183
    orange chocolate cake 181
    pistachio and chocolate squares 187
cannellini bean casserole 158
cannellini bean spaghetti 44
cannelloni 138
carrot pancakes, houmous and salad 103
cashew nut cookies 176
channa dhal 62
cheese
    cheese on toast 28
    chickpea and feta salad 39
    ciabatta goat's cheese salad 42
    creamy parmesan-style pasta 167
    goat's cheese tart with black olives 120
    leek and potato frittata with salad 72
    mushroom and brie pasta 164
    nachos 144
    peppers stuffed with feta and pine nuts 170
    salad tortillas with feta 52
    spinach and cheese rice slice 48
    spinach and cottage cheese lasagna 146
    two cheese and spinach loaf 140
cheese on toast 28
cheesy croutons 55
cherry cookies 178
cherry tomatoes and spaghetti 45
chestnut hot pot 151
chickpea and feta salad 39
chickpea patties with yogurt dressing 134
chickpeas with spinach 84
chilli bean stew, with crusty bread 161
chilli courgette torte 109
chilli egg fried rice 104
chilli tofu 125
chilli with aduki beans 85
chocolate cake 181
chocolate krispy munchies 188
chocolate truffles 186
ciabatta goat's cheese salad 42
classic nut roast 156
coconut veggies 53
coleslaw 129
cookies
    cherry cookies 178
corn cakes & ratatouille 98
courgette slice 116
couscous
    fried halloumi salad
        with pine nut couscous 127
    roast sweet potatoes with couscous and balsamic
        dressing 74
creamy parmesan-style pasta 167
croutons 39
crumble 94 193
curried split pea casserole 157
curried wedges 150
curry
    aubergine and coconut curry 87
    curried split pea casserole 157
    greek style egg curry 64
    korma beans with naan 107
    korma rice and spinach 76
    quorn madras curry 67

squash and apple curry 86

D

desserts
  apple crumble 193
  baked apples 192
  berry trifle 199
  bread and butter pud 195
  fruit fool 197
  fruity rice 196
  tiramisu 191
dipping salsa 145
dream bars 173

E

eans with naan 107
egg curry 64
eggs 30
  boiled eggs 30
  eggs 30
  greek style egg curry 64
  leek and potato frittata with salad 72
  mexican eggs 49
  no pastry quiche 92
  omelettes 31
  poached eggs 30
  scrambled eggs 30
  spanish baked eggs 131
eton mess 194

F

feta caesar salad 171
feta salad 39
french onion soup 55
fried halloumi salad
with pine nut couscous 127
fruit fool 197
fruit'n nut salad 130
fruity rice 196

G

goats cheese pancakes 46
goat's cheese salad 42
goat's cheese tart with black olives 120
good buying ideas 8
good things to eat 12
gratin
  leek and potato gratin 77
greek style egg curry 64
green pesto pasta with broccoli 43
green veg risotto 79

H

halloumi rosti 65
halloumi salad
with pine nut couscous 127
hoisin wrap 142
honey cake 177
honey mushroom and rice pie 101
hot pot 159
how long can i keep this before it kills me? 16

how to cook pasta 23
hummus 141

I

interesting sandwiches 26
introduction 3

J

jacket potato
  cheese and mushroom 24
  cheesy chives 24
  egg and mayo and sweetcorn 24
  roasted veg 24
  the simplest 24

K

khitcherie 90
koftas with mango yogurt dip 136
korma beans with naan 107
korma rice and spinach 76

L

lasagna 132
leek and potato frittata with salad 72
leek and potato gratin 77
leek and potato soup 155
lentil and apricot soup 59
lime and coconut drizzle cake 182

M

madras curry 67
mango and noodle salad 128
mediterranean bulghar wheat salad 117
melon, strawberries and yogurt smoothie 34
menus and shopping lists 200
mexican eggs 49
muffins 174
mug 4
mushroom and brie pasta 164
mushroom stroganoff 166

N

nachos 144
noodles
  rice noodles 105
no pastry quiche 92
nut and carrot coleslaw 129
nut and courgette slice 116
nut roast 156
nuts
  apple and cashew soup 57
  biryani with yogurt and cashews 69
  bubble & squeak 91
  cashew nut cookies 176
  classic nut roast 156
  fried halloumi salad with pine nut couscous 127
  fruit'n nut salad 130
  khitcherie 90
  nut and carrot coleslaw 129
  nut and courgette slice 116

nutty crumble 94
nutty fruit bars 179
nutty honey cake 177
nutty sweet potato and spinach pie 152
peppers stuffed with feta and pine nuts 170
pineapple and pine nut salad 41
potato and nut terrine 113 115
sweet potato and pecan salad 40
nut terrine 113 115
nutty crumble 94
nutty fruit bars 179
nutty honey cake 177
nutty sweet potato and spinach pie 152

O

oat crunchies 183
omelettes 31
onion and squash pie 118
orange and lemon buns 185
orange chocolate cake 181
orange smoothie 34

P

pancakes 198
   goats cheese pancakes 46
   savoury pancakes 122
parsnip and swede bake 110
pasta
   basic stir-fry 80
   cannelloni 138
   creamy parmesan-style pasta 167
   green pesto pasta with broccoli 43
   how to cook pasta 23
   mango and noodle salad 128
   mushroom and brie pasta 164
   pasta with onions and green beans 165
   pasta with roast vegetables 89
   quick veggie pasta 51
   spinach and cottage cheese lasagna 146
   tagliatelle with red pesto 47
pasta with onions and green beans 165
pasta with roast vegetables 89
peanut sauce 33
pecan salad 40
pepper sauce 32
peppers stuffed with feta and pine nuts 170
perfect rice every time 22
persian pilaf 143
pesto pasta with broccoli 43
pie
   onion and squash pie 118
pilaf 143
pineapple and pine nut salad 41
pine nut and pineapple salad 41
piquant dressing 37
piquant tomato sauce 32
pistachio and chocolate squares 187
pistachio hummus 141
poached eggs 30
potato
   bubble and squeak 91
   curried wedges 150
   jacket potato 24

leek and potato frittata with salad 72
leek and potato soup 155
nutty sweet potato and spinach pie 152
potato and nut terrine 113 115
potato hash 61
potato pan cake 50
roast sweet potatoes with couscous and balsamic
   dressing 74
roast wedges 149
shepherd's pie 160
spinach, bean and potato bake 112
sweet potato patties 93
sweet potato tagine 70
potato and leek frittata with salad 72
potato and nut terrine 113 115
potato hash 61
potato pan cake 50
potential pitfalls 15
pumpkin risotto 79

Q

quick cheese sauce 33
quick veggie pasta 51
quorn chilli with aduki beans 85
quorn madras curry 67

R

ratatouille 98
recipe costs 3
red chilli tofu 125
reheating & storing 17
rice
   basic risotto 78
   green veg risotto 79
   honey mushroom and rice pie 101
   korma rice and spinach 76
   perfect rice every time 22
   spanish risotto 79
   spicy pumpkin risotto 79
   spinach and cheese rice slice 48
   sweet and spicy pilau 111
   thai coconut veggies 53
rice noodles 105
risotto 78
roast cherry tomatoes and spaghetti 45
roasting veggies 21
roast sweet potatoes with couscous and balsamic
   dressing 74
roast tomato and halloumi salad 96
roast vegetable with chunky tofu 124
roast wedges 149
rosti 65

S

salad
   apple and bean salad 60
   carrot pancakes, houmous and salad 103
   chickpea and feta salad 39
   ciabatta goat's cheese salad 42
   feta caesar salad 171
   fried halloumi salad 74
   with pine nut couscous 127

fruit'n nut salad 130
mango and noodle salad 128
mediterranean bulghar wheat salad 117
pineapple and pine nut salad 41
roast tomato and halloumi salad 96
salad tortillas with feta 52
sweet potato and pecan salad 40
salad dressings 36
coconut dressing 36
creamy paprika dressing 36
french dressing 36
honey and lemon dressing 36
piquant dressing 37
raspberry and balsamic dressing 37
salad dressings 36
yogurt dressing 37
salad tortillas with feta 52
salsa
avocado salsa 145
dipping salsa 145
salsa 145
tomato and onion salsa 145
sandwiches 26
sauces 32
baked patties with chilli sauce 66
peanut sauce 33
pepper sauce 32
piquant tomato sauce 32
quick cheese sauce 33
sauces 32
sweet and sour sauce 32
tomato sauce 33
savoury pancakes 122
scrambled eggs 30
seven steps to success 18
shepherd's pie 160
simple key 3
smoothies 34
banana, honey and yogurt 34
melon, strawberries and yogurt smoothie 34
orange smoothie 34
strawberry smoothie 34
summer fruit smoothie 34
soups
apple and cashew soup 57
french onion soup 55
leek and potato soup 155
lentil and apricot soup 59
sweetcorn soup 58
tomato and lentil soup 56
spaghetti
cannellini bean spaghetti 44
roast cherry tomatoes and spaghetti 45
spaghetti bolognese 108
spaghetti bolognese 108
spanish baked eggs 131
spanish risotto 79
spicy chickpeas with spinach 84
spicy pumpkin risotto 79
spinach and cheese rice slice 48
spinach and cottage cheese lasagna 146
spinach, bean and potato bake 112
split pea casserole 157
squash and apple curry 86

stir-fry 80
basic stir-fry 80
cashews and vegetables 83
creamy vegetables 83
spinach 82
tomato with vegetables 82
storecupboard and fridge 10
strawberry smoothie 34
stroganoff 166
stuffed aubergines 163
stuffed peppers 170
stuff on taost 28
beans on toast with egg on top 28
cheese on toast 28
welsh rarebit 28
stuff on toast 28
summer fruit smoothie 34
sweet and sour quorn 168
sweet and sour sauce 32
sweet and spicy pilau 111
sweetcorn soup 58
sweet potato and pecan salad 40
sweet potato and spinach pie 152
sweet potato patties 93
sweet potato tagine 70

T

tagine 70
tagliatelle with red pesto 47
thai coconut veggies 53
things to look out for 14
tiramisu 191
tofu
red chilli tofu 125
roast vegetable with chunky tofu 124
tofu balls with tomato sauce 123
tofu balls with tomato sauce 123
tomato and lentil soup 56
tomato and onion salsa 145
tomato sauce 33
tortillas with feta 52
trifle 199
truffles 186
two cheese and spinach loaf 140

V

veggie bake with tomato sauce 100
veggie pasta 51
veggies 20
boiling veggies 20
roasting veggies 21
veggies 20
veg risotto 79

W

wedges 149
weekly food planner 9
welsh rarebit 28
what do i do if... 19
white chocolate cherry fudge 184
winter warming hot pot 159
wrap hoisin 142
wraps 148

REGISTER

at noshbooks.com/students to get vegetarian **student recipes** emailed to you every month

Why not join us LIVE on Periscope, where we experiment with new recipes all the time - @noshbooks

 Periscope

thanks...

This book would not have been possible without the help of many people. My husband Ron and my sons, Ben and Tim, have worked tirelessly to help me.

Thanks again to my very good friends, Fran, for her wonderful proof-reading and to Cathryn, for her help in the kitchen.

Many others came to collect and eat food on our photography days. Without them, much food would have been wasted, which is never a good thing!

Thanks to Tim and Ben's friends who have allowed us to use their faces for the front cover. Your free copy is on it's way!

Josh Smith, Katy Bosanko, Josh Feben, Daniella Clements, Deb Smith, Andy Tiffen, Tommy Andrewartha, Phil Hatton, Felix Page, Jo Skinner, Joel Bennett, Michael Pearce, Rav Hayer, Patrick Wilson, Kat Thomas, Jan Moys, Calum Maciver, Rachel Tiffen, Marianne Matthews, Emma Page, Michelle Crispin, Gareth Matthews, Payin Swazey Attafuah, Mary-Jane Attafuah, Chester See, Ems Smith, Jon Herring, Charlie Gregson, Nathanael Bennett, Paul Cannon, James Malbon, Jess Whitbread, Tom Whitbread, Tim Crispin, Naomi Badu, Rach Clements, Hannah Clements, Naomi Clements, Nathaniel Ledwidge, Tekiva Ledwidge, Peter Kent, Beccy Catley, Matt Bentley, Nicola Goodwin, Leanne Clack, Trudy Willoughby, Cerys Duffty, Amy Banham-Hall, Jonathan Ingham, Tom Povey, Nicole May, Emily Malbon, Ross Macfarlane, Amy Macfarlane, Kirsty Macfarlane, Richard Wells, Juliet Adekambi, Simon William Burns, Sharon Makinde, Rachel Donley, Hannah Rich, Nathan Clements, Rachel Phillipps, Odele Caldecourt, Ben McCalla, Dan Richter, Jon Povey, Peter Goult, Connie Haywood, Jez Hill, Ed Gent, Jenny Copperwheat, Dan Copperwheat, Clarence Bissessar, Sarju Patel, Chris Low, Gabbie D'Mello, Esther Gore, Polly West, Kerry Cannon, Kirsty Crooks, Gareth Paton, Lizzie De Kraan, Jonathan Cannon, Matt Skinner, Luke Clements, Lizzie Fieldsend, Leland Fieldsend and Paul Summerville

Published by: Intrade (GB) Ltd

Contact: joymay@mac.com

Author: Joy May

Printed in China

1st Edition: 2006
2nd Edition: March 2011
Revised 2nd Edition: June 2013
3rd Edition: May 2017
2nd Print: September 2017

ISBN: 9780993260940

Photography: Milk Bottle Photography

Design: Milk Bottle Designs

Proof-reading: Fran Maciver

Editor: Ron May